ISSUES THAT CONCERN YOU

Gun Violence

Lauri S. Scherer, *Book Editor*

GREENHAVEN PRESS
A part of Gale, Cengage Learning

GALE
CENGAGE Learning·

Detroit • New York • San Francisco • New Haven, Conn • Waterville, Maine • London

GALE
CENGAGE Learning®

Elizabeth Des Chenes, *Director, Publishing Solutions*

© 2013 Greenhaven Press, a part of Gale, Cengage Learning

Gale and Greenhaven Press are registered trademarks used herein under license.

For more information, contact:
Greenhaven Press
27500 Drake Rd.
Farmington Hills, MI 48331-3535
Or you can visit our Internet site at gale.cengage.com

Articles in Greenhaven Press anthologies are often edited for length to meet page requirements. In addition, original titles of these works are changed to clearly present the main thesis and to explicitly indicate the author's opinion. Every effort is made to ensure that Greenhaven Press accurately reflects the original intent of the authors. Every effort has been made to trace the owners of copyrighted material.

Cover image © Corbis Premium RF/Alamy

LIBRARY OF CONGRESS CATALOGING-IN-PUBLICATION DATA

Gun violence / Lauri S. Scherer, book editor.
   p. cm. -- (Issues that concern you)
 Includes bibliographical references and index.
 ISBN 978-0-7377-6295-2 (hardcover)
1. Gun control--United States. 2. Firearms and crime--United States. 3. Violent crimes--United States. 4. Firearms ownership--Government policy--United States.
I. Scherer, Lauri S.
 HV7436.G876 2012
 363.330973--dc23
                            2012015800

Printed in the United States of America
1 2 3 4 5 6 7 16 15 14 13 12

CONTENTS

Introduction   5

1. **Guns Cause Violence**   9
   Harold Evans

2. **Guns Prevent Violence**   14
   Michael Reagan

3. **Gun Violence Is the Product of a Sick Society**   19
   David A. Love

4. **A Society Without Guns Is Sick**   24
   Skip Coryell

5. **Gun Violence Particularly Threatens
   African Americans**   29
   Violence Policy Center

6. **Gun Violence Particularly Threatens Women**   34
   Alice Dahle

7. **Gun Violence Particularly Threatens Children**   39
   Children's Defense Fund

8. **Widespread Gun Ownership Puts Police at Risk**   48
   Brady Center to Prevent Gun Violence

9. **Civilian Gun Ownership Helps Police
   Fight Crime**   53
   John Stossel

10. **Tighter Gun Control Laws Can Reduce
    Gun Violence**   58
    USA Today

11. **Gun Control Laws Restrict Those Least Likely
    to Commit Violence**   63
    Don B. Kates Jr.

12. **Reinstate Ban on Military-Style Assault Weapons**   67
Arizona Daily Star

13. **Assault Weapons Should Not Be Banned**   72
Jacob Hornberger

14. **People Should Be Allowed to Carry
Guns in Bars**   77
Washington Times

15. **People Should Not Be Allowed to Carry
Guns in Bars**   80
Toledo Blade

16. **People Should Be Allowed to Carry Guns
in Churches**   84
Scott McPherson

17. **Pastoral Guidance on Conceal and Carry Law**   89
Archdiocese of Milwaukee

18. **Schools Should Be Gun-Free Zones**   93
Colin Goddard

19. **Schools Should Not Be Gun-Free Zones**   97
Philip Harris

Appendix

What You Should Know About Gun Violence   102
What You Should Do About Gun Violence   107

Organizations to Contact   110

Bibliography   115

Index   120

Picture Credits   126

INTRODUCTION

The United States has a long and complicated history with guns. The experience of needing to fight, violently, for their freedom and their rights led the nation's founders to enshrine within the Constitution the Second Amendment, which famously states: "A well regulated militia, being necessary to the security of a free state, the right of the people to keep and bear arms, shall not be infringed."

More than 235 years later, the founders would be interested to know that there are nearly as many guns as there are people in the United States they helped create. According to the Brady Campaign to Prevent Gun Violence, there are about 283 million guns in the hands of a population comprising about 300 million people. That works out to about 88 guns per 100 people, which, according to the Small Arms Survey, is the highest rate of gun ownership in the world. Of course, 88 percent of the population does not own a gun, as gun ownership is highly concentrated. About 20 percent of gun owners own 65 percent of the nation's guns, or, put another way, about 25 percent of adults own one or more guns. Each year, about 4.5 million new firearms, including approximately 2 million handguns, are sold in the United States, and about 2 million secondhand firearms are sold each year as well.

Society is saturated with guns, and advocates and opponents of gun control (that is, laws and policies designed to regulate the sale, ownership, and use of guns) interpret this same fact in diametrically opposed ways. For some, the high volume of guns is directly responsible for the unacceptably high level of gun violence. For others, the high volume of guns is precisely the reason Americans need to be armed: to protect themselves and their families from armed criminals who mean them harm. Whether guns are the cause of or antidote to gun violence is a core and critical question, with no clear answer.

An oft-made point by gun control opponents is that armed citizens are in the best position to stop, or at least minimize, gun violence at a crime scene until police get there. There are many examples of times in which guns helped cut short shooting sprees, prevent further loss of life, or hold a criminal at bay until police arrived on the scene. Conservative commentator and talk show host Larry Elder recounts a couple of them:

> Edinboro, Pennsylvania. A 14-year-old middle school student opened fire at a school graduation dance, being held at a local restaurant. The shooter killed one teacher and wounded two students and another teacher. The armed teenager was apprehended by the restaurant owner, who grabbed his own shotgun from his office and went after the shooter. Staring into the owner's shotgun, the teen dropped his gun and surrendered.

> Pearl, Mississippi. A 16-year-old sophomore entered Pearl High with a hunting rifle under his overcoat. He opened fire, killing two students and wounding seven. The assistant principal, Joel Myrick, ran to his truck and retrieved the .45 automatic he kept there. Running back, he spotted the shooter in the parking lot. Ordering the teen to stop, the vice principal put his gun to the shooter's neck and held him until police arrived.[1]

Elder and others argue that being without a gun in a criminal situation leaves people unable to defend themselves. Moreover, when criminals know people do not have guns, they may be more likely to commit crime, because they are confident they will not be challenged. In fact, one study conducted by the National Institute of Justice found that 74 percent of polled felons said that robbers tend to avoid stealing from houses when people are home because they do not want to be shot at. The assumption that a homeowner might own a gun, therefore, theoretically can prevent a crime.

Yet gun control supporters find it difficult to avoid the logic that if guns are used to violent ends, then fewer, not more, of

The April 2012 fatal shooting of seventeen-year-old Trayvon Martin in Sanford, Florida, led to a renewed discussion of gun violence in the United States.

them is the solution to reducing gun violence. "Guns kill people," states columnist Harold Evans unequivocally. "A single gun can kills lots of them in seconds. A single knife can't. The gun has a unique utility for translating rage into instant killing."[2]

Moreover, Evans and others point out that simply having a gun does not necessarily stop crime nor make a person immune to being a victim. Consider the events of January 8, 2011, when Jared Lee Loughner shot US Representative Gabrielle Giffords and twelve other people while they met to discuss political issues outside a supermarket near Tucson, Arizona. Arizona has some of the highest gun ownership rates and some of the least restrictive gun control policies in the nation, and yet one of the country's worst shootings happened amid this heavily armed citizenry. "I would have thought that if there was anywhere this was least likely to occur, it was Arizona," said John McGinness, a former Sacramento County, California, sheriff.[3] "When the bullets started flying, experienced gun owners became victims of violence like anybody else," says Marcus Breton, a gun owner who was forced to rethink guns' role in preventing violence after the Tucson shootings. "The incident proves that guns don't make you bulletproof."[4]

Whether guns are the cause of or antidote to gun violence is among the many topics explored in *Issues That Concern You: Gun Violence*. Readers will consider opposing perspectives on questions ranging from whether guns cause violence or prevent violence; what kinds of guns, if any, should be banned; who is most affected by gun violence; where guns should be allowed; and other key issues surrounding this perennial social debate.

Notes

1. Larry Elder, "Do 'Gun-Free' Zones Encourage School Shootings?," *Human Events*, October 18, 2007. www.human events.com/article.php?id=22911.
2. Harold Evans, "Arizona Shootings: Tell the Victims That Guns Don't Kill," DailyBeast.com. January 10, 2011. www.the dailybeast.com/articles/2011/01/10/arizona-shootings-tell-the -victims-that.html.
3. Quoted in Marcus Breton, "Gun Violence Won't Be Prevented by More Gun Ownership," *Sacramento (CA) Bee*, January 16, 2011. www.mcclatchydc.com/2011/01/16/106651/commentary -gun-violence-wont-be.html.
4. Breton, "Gun Violence Won't Be Prevented by More Gun Ownership."

ONE

Guns Cause Violence

Harold Evans

In the following viewpoint, Harold Evans argues that
access to guns enables people to kill others quickly,
efficiently, and disastrously. He takes issue with the
mantra, "Guns don't kill people, people kill people." In
Evans's opinion, this way of thinking excuses those who
oppose reasonable gun-control laws. He argues that of
course guns kill people, and they do so more effectively
and from further away than knives or other weapons.
He cites statistics that show places with more guns and
gun ownership experience higher homicide rates. He
concludes that politicians and other leaders must not
ignore the role guns play in violent crime and that
they must acknowledge the connection between guns
and death.

Evans, a knight of the British realm and the former editor of the *Times* of London, is the author of two histories
of the United States, as well as a personal memoir.

Blaming [the January 8, 2011, shootings in] Tucson[1] on the vile language in public discourse is a cop out. The crucial issue is not language. It is law. We are supposed to be a nation of laws but Democrats and Republicans alike run away from laws that would curtail the killings. They'll now talk endlessly about civility, about which faction is coarser. And if they do get round to the bullets that do the killing, it's a sure bet we'll get only the routine bromides.

Guns don't kill people . . .

You will hear that for weeks now. It's a line crafted by the National Rifle Association [NRA], chanted by ditto heads after every tragic shooting, every massacre.

People Use Guns to Kill

"It is not that the gun was evil, but that it was in the hands of an evil person," Rep. Trent Franks (R-AZ) assures us on *Meet the Press*. Echoes the Tea Party's Sen. Mike Lee (R-UT) on CNN: No laws curtailing gun ownership could stop a person "bent on performing evil acts to kill another person."

Is that so? If the *Tucson madman did not easily and legally acquire his gun* and the large magazine of bullets with it, would he have been able to vent his evil on a crowd of people, killing at least six and wounding 13?

A Powerful Killing Tool

Of course not. Guns kill people. A single gun can kills lots of them in seconds. A single knife can't. The gun has a unique utility for translating rage into instant killing. The gunman can kill at a distance or get close, concealing the weapon, and take the victims by surprise. The counterargument is that if a victim has a gun, the gunman won't try. There is something in that. But the attacker always

---

1. Gunman Jared Lee Loughner opened fire on a political gathering in front of an Arizona supermarket, killing six people, including a federal judge, and wounding thirteen others, including Congresswoman Gabrielle Giffords.

has the benefit of surprise. Sadly, it didn't help Rep. Gabrielle Giffords that she is a gun owner and a keen Second Amendment supporter. Banks are well-defended but still get robbed.

The chant that guns don't kill people is just a cowardly way of evading responsibility for making a six-death nightmare of Rep. Giffords' attempt to hear from her constituents, for ending the career of a fine federal judge, for carelessly ending the young life of 9-year-old Christina Green, who was intent on learning more about how America governs itself.

This is how, Christina.

The Truth About Guns in America

By evading a sensible debate on controlling gun violence, by smearing everyone who dares to raise the issue as a liberal bent

Paramedics aid a shooting victim outside a Tucson, Arizona, shopping center where Jared Loughner shot and killed six people on January 8, 2011, and wounded US Congresswoman Gabrielle Giffords and twelve others.

on subverting the Second Amendment, by gymnastic feats of illogic to explain away certain facts:

- That all the comparable Western countries with reasonable gun-control laws have long had far fewer gun homicides. The murder rate per 100,000 for the U.S. is 5.28. For Canada, it is 0.47, for Australia it is 0.07, the U.K. 0.06, and Japan 0.05.
- That the murder rate in the U.S. correlates very closely with the sale of firearms. More guns mean more deaths, and gun ownership has outpaced increases in population.
- That the states with the most porous gun laws and highest gun ownership—Louisiana, Alaska, Alabama, Nevada—have the nation's highest per capita gun death rates, according to the 2007 data from federal studies released by the Violence Policy Center. Conversely, states with lower rates of gun ownership and stronger laws had far fewer gun deaths. Best states for staying alive: Hawaii, followed by Rhode Island, Massachusetts,

More Guns, More Death

According to analysis by the Violence Policy Center, states with higher gun ownership rates and weak gun laws have the highest rates of gun death. By contrast, states with strong gun laws and low rates of gun ownership have far lower rates of firearm-related death.

Rank	State	Household Gun Ownership Percentage	Gun Death Rate per 100,000	Rank	State	Household Gun Ownership Percentage	Gun Death Rate per 100,000
	States with the Five Highest Gun-Death Rates				**States with the Five Lowest Gun-Death Rates**		
1	Alaska	60.6	20.64	50	Hawaii	9.7	3.18
2	Mississippi	54.3	19.32	49	Massachusetts	12.8	3.42
3	Louisiana	45.6	18.47	48	Rhode Island	13.3	4.18
4	Alabama	57.2	17.53	47	New York	18.1	4.95
5	Wyoming	62.8	17.45	46	New Jersey	11.3	4.95

Taken from: Violence Policy Center, October 2011.

Connecticut, and New York. If you live in Nevada, you are three times more likely to die from firearms than if you live in New York.

- That the keenest advocates of reasonable—repeat reasonable—gun laws are the police. Police chiefs are baffled that the NRA and the puppet members of Congress block the measures that would help the police trace murder weapons and close the gun-show loophole by which criminals and unstable people get their hands on weapons of mass murder.

Politicians Must Lead and Protect

The cowardice of the politicians is wondrous to behold. During the 2008 presidential campaign, President [Barack] Obama and his attorney general both promised to reintroduce the ban on assault weapons. Once elected, they fled the scene. Like so many in Congress, of both parties, they are scared of the NRA. But is the NRA membership as extremist as its leadership that routinely exercises its unscrupulous ability to whip up hysteria?

The 500 mayors in the national coalition of Mayors Against Illegal Guns commissioned a study by conservative pollster Frank Luntz to test the views of 401 NRA members and 431 gun owners who are not members.

Two of his questions produced surprising answers:

1. Would you support or oppose requiring gun sellers at gun shows to conduct criminal background checks?

Answer: 69 percent of NRA members would and 85 percent of gun owners who are not members.

2. Do you agree or disagree with this statement: "The federal government should not restrict the police's ability to access, use, and share data that helps them enforce federal, state, and local gun laws."

Answer: Of NRA members, 69 percent agreed there should be no restrictions and 74 percent of the others.

Maybe the NRA is the Wizard of Oz [that is, a scary image with little behind it]. The appalling shootings in Tucson are a chance to find out.

TWO

Guns Prevent Violence

Michael Reagan

In the following viewpoint, political consultant Michael Reagan discusses how on July 23, 2011, Norwegian Anders Behring Breivik killed seventy-six people during twin terrorist attacks. A main reason Breivik's rampage was so deadly, says Reagan, is because Norwegian citizens are not allowed to carry guns. Therefore, no one could shoot Breivik to stop him or corner him with a weapon to make him surrender. In Reagan's view, Breivik had all the power because he had the best weapon—no one could defend against him. Criminals feel emboldened when they know their victims will be unarmed; on the other hand, criminals will think more carefully about their actions if they know they are likely to be shot themselves, contends Reagan. He concludes that allowing people to have guns empowers them to prevent crime and reduce fatalities when terrorists like Breivik strike.

Reagan is the son of former president Ronald Reagan.

How long would the Norway gunman have lasted in Texas or any state where concealed-carry laws are on the books? I ran a survey while on a cruise: in Texas, 3 minutes; in Montana, 7 to 8 minutes; in Arizona, 2 minutes; and in Nevada, 3 to 5 minutes.

Author Michael Reagan (pictured) contends that if Norwegians were allowed to carry guns, mass murderer Anders Behring Breivik would not have killed so many people, and the massacre might even have been prevented.

Had Norway not surrendered to the anti–self-defense nuts, and allowed Norwegians to protect themselves by legally carrying guns, the massacre might well have been prevented. There's a lot of truth in the old adage that if guns are outlawed only outlaws will carry guns.

Moreover, if anyone had paid attention to [Anders Behring] Breivik's[1] rants they would not have been surprised when he acted on them, especially since Breivik had preceded his attack by setting off a car bomb in the heart of Oslo.

1. On July 23, 2011, Breivik killed seventy-six people in a shooting spree in Norway.

Tragically, Norway's anti-gun hysteria resulted in laws restricting gun ownership by law-abiding citizens, leaving them exposed to gun violence at the hands of criminals such as Breivik, who simply ignore anti-gun ownership laws. Despite the Second Amendment, which protects American citizens' rights to access to guns for self-protection, the Constitutional right of citizens to bear arms is under constant assault.

The Defenseless Are Easier to Rule

In his best-selling classic *More Guns, Less Crime*, John R. Lott, Jr. has proven that guns make us safer. And in the book *The Bias against Guns*, he shows how liberals bury pro-gun facts out of sheer bias against the truth. With irrefutable evidence, Lott shot down gun critics and provided information we need to win arguments with those fanatics who want to ban gun ownership, leaving criminals who ignore anti-gun ownership laws armed.

History teaches us that governments faced with an armed citizenry are restrained from usurping the rights of individuals. It is thus no surprise that governments which seek to exercise dictatorial powers over their citizens inevitably seek to restrict or outlaw gun ownership by their citizenry.

More Guns Equals Less Crime

In an interview with the University of Chicago, Lott said that states with the largest increases in gun ownership also have the largest drops in violent crimes. Thirty-one states now have such laws—called "shall-issue" laws. These laws allow adults the right to carry concealed handguns if they do not have a criminal record or a history of significant mental illness.

He noted that criminals are deterred by higher penalties. Just as higher arrest and conviction rates deter crime, so does the risk that someone committing a crime will confront someone able to defend him or herself. He shows that there is a strong negative relationship between the number of law-abiding citizens who have gun permits and the crime rate, noting that as more people obtain permits there is a greater decline in violent crime rates. He adds that for each additional year that a concealed handgun law is in effect the murder rate declines by 3 percent, rape by 2 percent, and robberies by over 2 percent.

The Best Defense

Concealed handgun laws reduce violent crime for two reasons. First, they reduce the number of attempted crimes because criminals are uncertain which potential victims can defend themselves.

Americans Strongly Support Gun Ownership

Question: "Do you think there should or should not be a law that would ban the possession of handguns, except by the police and other authorized persons?"

% Should be   % Should not be

Taken from: Gallup Organization, "Record-Low 26% in U.S. Favor Handgun Ban," October 26, 2011.

Second, victims who have guns are in a much better position to defend themselves. That's just common sense.

Our Founding Fathers understood the need for an armed citizenry. Thanks to the colonists who were armed, America triumphed over the strongest army in the world. They insisted that their fellow Americans have a right to bear arms in order to guarantee their liberties and safeguard them from those who would deny them the freedom they won on the battlefields of the American Revolution.

We need to be ever vigilant—there are always those who would trample on our rights as free Americans. As long as we retain the right to self-defense guaranteed by the right to own and bear arms, our freedoms will be secure.

THREE

Gun Violence Is the Product of a Sick Society

David A. Love

In the following viewpoint, David A. Love suggests that American society is sick for having normalized gun violence. He explains that shootings follow a predictable cycle: Someone kills others at a school or place of business; people debate why and then go on with their lives. Love laments that no one sees this as a critical problem or something in immediate need of preventing. He suggests that Americans have become too willing to tolerate gun violence in society. He argues that a society that lives with random, violent shootings can never be free, stable, or vibrant. He concludes that Americans suffer from a sickness that can only be cured by becoming unwilling to tolerate any further death.

Love, a writer and human rights activists, is on the editorial board of BlackCommentator.com and also contributes to The Progressive Media Project.

Sadly, it's the sort of thing that happens on a regular basis these days. Someone, whether a disgruntled employee, a mentally unstable individual, a socially-awkward or obsessive person, you fill in the blank, goes on a shooting spree and exacts vengeance through the barrel of a gun. People express shock that this sort of thing could happen where they live, in the safe environs far from the nation's notoriously crime-ridden inner cities. Some will claim there were no indications the shooting suspect was capable of such violence. Meanwhile, others will insist "there was always something off" about the person. In any case, after the obligatory media coverage and perfunctory surface-level discussions, after the memorials are held, the grief counselors are dispatched and the victims are buried, things generally go back to normal. All is forgotten, that is, until the next tragic shooting that leaves x number of people dead and y number of people injured.

It was said that Amy Bishop,[1] that biology professor at the University of Alabama–Huntsville was angry because she had been denied tenure by the university. She supposedly visited a shooting range before her shooting rampage. And she was obsessed with President [Barack] Obama. We also know that she shot her brother to death years earlier in what was ruled as an accidental killing, and she was a suspect in an attempted pipe bombing of her professor at Harvard.

Always Reacting, Never Preventing

There are questions that are beyond the scope of this commentary, but deserve some mention nonetheless. We know that the three victims who died, allegedly at her hand, were faculty of color. Was this deliberate? Certainly there is a story hidden in there, somewhere. Had Amy Bishop been a person of color herself—perhaps an African American, or a Muslim with an Arab surname—would she have eluded the institutional screeners and gatekeepers for so long, given her sketchy past? Was she given a pass because she is white, despite her issues? Perhaps for some, these are insensitive questions to ask at this time, or any other time for that matter, but ask I must.

Oddly and consistently, such questions are always raised after the fact. You never hear of a shooting rampage that was thwarted, with the perpetrator-to-be either apprehended or otherwise

1. On February 12, 2010, Bishop stood up at a university biology department meeting and shot at colleagues, killing three of them.

Police escort university professor Amy Bishop to court in 2011. Bishop is accused of killing three people during a shooting rampage at the University of Alabama–Huntsville in 2010.

stopped in his or her (generally his) tracks. Never do we hear of an intervention that allows such troubled individuals to receive the counseling and treatment they need, to protect themselves, and us, from the demons that haunt them.

Why Do We Tolerate Death?

And yet, while we will dismiss the perpetrators of such vicious acts as criminals or mentally disturbed outliers, our response to these tragedies reveals far more about our sick society than the troubled souls who committed the crimes. *Tens of thousands of people* die from gunfire in America every year, and most never get media attention. And yet, in a nation that has normalized the notion of a gun for every person, this is apparently a situation we are willing to tolerate. Based on the lack of an adequate public policy response to America's gun problem, one must conclude

Gun Ownership Around the World

The data below compares civilian gun ownership per 100 civilians in the United States with civilian gun ownership per 100 civilians in a sampling of other countries. The US rate is highest.

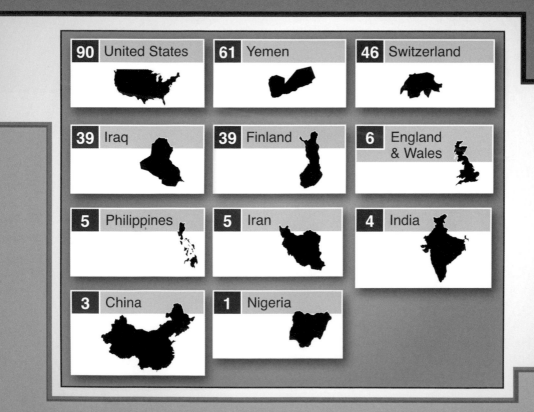

90 United States
61 Yemen
46 Switzerland
39 Iraq
39 Finland
6 England & Wales
5 Philippines
5 Iran
4 India
3 China
1 Nigeria

Taken from: Graduate Institute of International Studies, Geneva/National Rifle Association/*Virginia-Pilot* (Norfolk, VA), Small Arms Survey, March 2, 2008.

that these firearm deaths are viewed as collateral damage, the price society is willing to pay for a so-called "free" society of gun ownership rights.

No one can believe that the level of violence, of gun violence, in the United States is compatible with a stable, vibrant and free society. Add to the mix the high level of hopelessly unemployed and (or) foreclosed citizens who lack an outlet to vent their frustrations; the legions of veterans of the Iraq and Afghanistan wars, who have returned home with undiagnosed or untreated post-traumatic stress disorder; and the use of prisons as a repository for the mentally ill, with inmates returning to the streets sicker than when they were on lockdown. Lots of guns, economic despair, deprivation and mental illness—these conditions are a recipe for disaster.

The Problem That Shoots Us in the Face

In short, we are sick, and we need good medicine. The nation's political leadership often has proven too cowardly or too compromised to provide anything more than band-aids, but the band-aids haven't worked. In a country with so many crises, gun violence is yet another problem we have avoided for too long, only to have it shoot us in the face. But we cannot ignore it anymore, and we must make it right.

FOUR

A Society Without Guns Is Sick

Skip Coryell

Without guns, society will break down into terrifying chaos, argues Skip Coryell in the following viewpoint. Coryell says the natural state of animals is that the strong dominate the weak, preying upon them to survive. Guns, on the other hand, give small, weaker humans the ability to defend themselves against stronger people. In his view, a gun helps a tiny woman defend herself against a rapist; a gun protects a peaceful family from a psychopathic burglar. For this reason, Coryell views guns as society's equalizing force because they level the playing field between all humans. Take them away, he warns, and there will be nothing but chaos and evil left.

Coryell is the founder of the Second Amendment March, a grassroots organization that supports Americans' right to own guns.

According to *Webster's New World College Dictionary*, the term "saber rattling" is defined as: *a threatening of war, or a menacing show of armed force*. Some people call it posturing. In the animal world it's related to establishing "pecking order." Some people would have us believe that a pecking order is a bad thing, that it's barbaric, and should be reserved only for the animal world. I disagree. It's a natural thing that will happen no matter how much people try to suppress it. Pecking order keeps the world in a state of organized cosmos. Every playground has one, every corporate board room, and even the halls of Congress. It's the way the world works, and without it there would be chaos and unending strife. People have to know who is in charge and who must bend the knee and kiss the ring that rules.

An Equalizing Force

I suppose that's why firearms are so important. They are the equalizing force, available to all free people everywhere. They tell the 200-pound sexually aggressive male that he must not rape the 120-pound female, who is alone on the street at night with no one around to protect her. The firearm gives her the ability to kill the stronger male. Firearms tell the sociopath that he must not break into your family's home at night and kill your family as you sleep. There is always the chance that you will awaken, get your firearm and shoot him until he dies. Dead sociopaths and dead rapists. That's a good thing, a necessary thing for society to function in an orderly fashion.

Without Guns, Chaos

Without the right to keep and bear arms, we revert to humanity's default state of "law of the jungle," where only the strong survive, where the big rule the small, and where the weak die in a puddle of blood, flesh and urine. We need the firearm and the freedom to use it or our children will live in a binary world of masters and slaves, with no check on immorality, no governor to hold the strong accountable, and no way to protect the weak from the strong.

In a world without freedom and firearms, only the evil will have guns, and they will use them to the detriment and enslavement of good people everywhere. History has taught us that, and it's a lesson we should forget only at our own peril. . . .

Proponents of gun ownership say guns give weaker people the ability to defend themselves against attack and can help prevent rapes and burglaries.

"I'd Just Go Ahead and Die!"

Several years ago, I was teaching a husband and wife in a private firearms class. We were on the range behind their barn, shooting at targets up against an embankment. The woman was shooting a nice, 9mm Glock, and she honestly could not hit the broad side of a barn from the inside. I tried everything I knew to get her on target, but it was no use. I couldn't find the problem. Her husband told me she was a good shot, and that she usually shot better than he did. I questioned her some more, and she finally threw up her hands in frustration and said, "I don't even know why I'm doing this! I could never shoot anyone anyways. My husband made me take this class!" At her remark, a light went off in my head, and I interjected, "What if someone was trying to kill you? Could you shoot someone then!" She said, "No! I couldn't kill someone to save my own life. I'd just go ahead and die!"

A Threat to Loved Ones

I thought that was rather odd, but I could tell she was sincere, so I thought about it a second, and then I said, "Okay, let's use a little training technique called visualization." She nodded her head impatiently. "Okay, here's the scenario: You're at the gas station filling your tank. A man drives up and parks next to your car. He gets out, walks over, reaches through the open window of your car, removes your daughter from her car seat and puts her in his own vehicle. He then starts to get into his car to drive away."

There was a horrified look on the young mother's face. "At that moment in time, could you take another human life?" Without hesitation, this proper Christian woman said, "I would kill that son of a bitch!"

I said, "Okay then, that target down there is the man who is stealing your daughter. Fire away." She never missed the target again.

Guns Keep Society in Check

My question to everyone reading this article is this: "For you, as an individual, when do you draw your saber? When do you say 'Yes, I am willing to rise up and overthrow an oppressive, totalitarian government?'"

Is it when the government takes away your private business?

Is it when the government rigs elections?

Is it when the government imposes martial law?

Is it when the government takes away your firearms?

Now, don't get me wrong. I'm not advocating the immediate use of force against the government. It isn't time, and hopefully that time will never come. But one thing is certain: "Now is the time to rattle your sabers." If not now, then when? When the government ignores the First Amendment, it is time to rattle the Second Amendment sabers. It's all about accountability. So

American Gun Ownership Is on the Decline

Data analyzed by the Violence Policy Center show that increasingly fewer households own guns. Opponents of gun control worry that an unarmed population will be more defenseless against criminals.

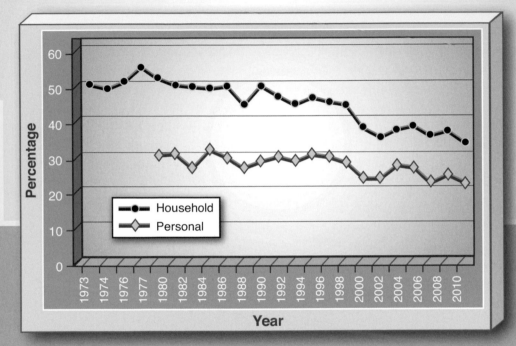

Taken from: General Social Survey conducted by the National Opinion Research Center (NORC) at the University of Chicago; analyzed by the Violence Policy Center, 2011.

long as our elected officials believe we will rise up and overthrow them under certain conditions, then they will not allow those conditions to occur. Their jobs and their very lives depend on it.

I understand that sounds harsh, but these are harsh times. Now is the time to rattle the saber. Now is the time to answer the very personal, very serious, very intimate question: "When do I remove the saber from its scabbard?" I hear the clank of metal on metal getting closer, but that's not enough. The politicians have to hear it too. They have to hear it, and they have to believe it.

FIVE

Gun Violence Particularly Threatens African Americans

Violence Policy Center

In the following report, the Violence Policy Center shows that gun violence particularly threatens African Americans. In just one year, guns were involved in the murders of more than fifty-three hundred black Americans and were a factor in 82 percent of all homicides in the black community. The author argues that black Americans are more and disproportionately affected by both homicide and gun violence than any other group. The author concludes that reducing access to guns could save thousands of African American lives each year.

The Violence Policy Center is a national educational foundation that works to enhance gun control in the United States.

America faces a continuing epidemic of homicide among young black males. From 2002 to 2007, the number of black male juvenile homicide victims rose by 31 percent. The number of young black homicide victims killed by guns rose at an even sharper rate: 54 percent. The devastation homicide inflicts on black teens and adults is a national crisis, yet it is all too often ignored outside of affected communities. . . .

Violence Policy Center, "Black Homicide Victimization in the United States: An Analysis of 2008 Homicide Data," January 2011. www.vpc.org.

Firearm Deaths of Children and Teens, by Race and Manner, 2007

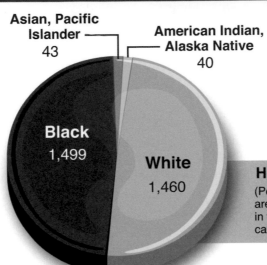

Asian, Pacific Islander
43

American Indian, Alaska Native
40

Black
1,499

White
1,460

TOTAL: 3,042

Hispanic 611
(Persons of Hispanic origin are not included separately in this pie chart because they can be of any race.)

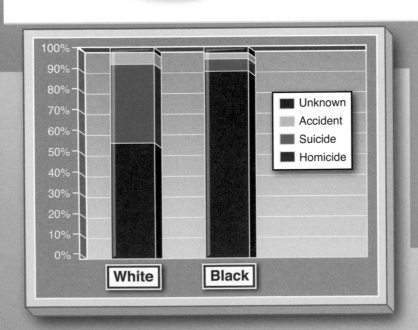

Unknown
Accident
Suicide
Homicide

White

Black

Taken from: US Department of Health and Human Services, Centers for Disease Control and Prevention, National Center for Injury Prevention and Control, WISQARS, *Protect Children, Not Guns*. www.cdc.gov/ncipc/wisqars. Calculations by Children's Defense Fund, 2010.

More Black than White Victims

According to the FBI SHR [Federal Bureau of Investigation *Supplementary Homicide Report*] data, in 2008 there were 6,841 black homicide victims in the United States. The homicide rate among black victims in the United States was 18.07 per 100,000. For that year, the overall national homicide rate was 4.93 per 100,000. For whites, the national homicide rate was 2.99 per 100,000. Additional information contained in the FBI SHR data on black homicide includes the following [statistics].

Of the 6,841 black homicide victims, 5,878 (86 percent) were male, and 961 (14 percent) were female. In two cases, the gender of the victim was unknown. The homicide rate for black male victims was 32.49 per 100,000. In comparison, the overall rate for male homicide victims was 7.93 per 100,000. For white male homicide victims it was 4.44 per 100,000. The homicide rate for black female victims was 4.86 per 100,000. In comparison, the overall rate for female homicide victims was 1.99 per 100,000. For white female homicide victims it was 1.57 per 100,000. Six hundred sixteen black homicide victims (9 percent) were less than 18 years old and 120 black homicide victims (2 percent) were 65 years of age or older. The average age was 30 years old.

Over 80 Percent Killed with Guns

For homicides in which the weapon used could be identified, 82 percent of black victims (5,308 out of 6,445) were shot and killed with guns. Of these, 72 percent (3,843 victims) were killed with handguns. There were 653 victims killed with knives or other cutting instruments, 248 victims killed by bodily force, and 150 victims killed by a blunt object.

For homicides in which the victim to offender relationship could be identified, 75 percent of black victims (2,398 out of 3,206) were murdered by someone they knew. Eight hundred eight victims were killed by strangers.

Blacks More Often Victims of Homicide

For homicides in which the circumstances could be identified, 71 percent (2,892 out of 4,099) were not related to the commission of any other felony. Of these, 56 percent (1,608 homicides) involved arguments between the victim and the offender. Eleven percent (330 homicides) were reported to be gang-related. Thirty-five percent of gang-related homicides (116 homicides) were in California, which may be in part due to more comprehensive reporting. In California, 46 percent of non-felony related homicides were reported to be gang-related.

In 2008, the national black homicide victimization rate was 18.07 per 100,000. For that year, Missouri ranked first as the state

Police in Oakland, California, investigate the shooting death of a twelve-year-old black youth. In 2008 there were 6,841 black homicide victims in the United States.

with the highest black homicide victimization rate. Its rate of 39.90 per 100,000 was more than double the national average for black homicide victims. . . . According to the SHR data, 17 states had a black homicide victimization rate higher than the national per capita rate of 18.07 per 100,000. . . . Blacks in the United States are disproportionately affected by homicide. For the year 2008, blacks represented 13 percent of the nation's population, yet accounted for 48 percent of all homicide victims.

Reducing Access to Guns Can Save Black Lives

As noted at the beginning of this study, the devastation homicide inflicts on black teens and adults is a national crisis, yet it is all too often ignored outside of affected communities. For blacks, like all victims of homicide, guns—usually handguns—are far and away the number one murder tool. Successful efforts to reduce America's black homicide toll must put a focus on reducing access and exposure to firearms.

SIX

Gun Violence Particularly Threatens Women

Alice Dahle

In the following viewpoint, Alice Dahle explains the ways in which gun violence uniquely affects women. She reports that guns are more likely to be owned by men and used against women, especially in cases of domestic violence. Dahle reports that around the world, guns are used to threaten, rape, and kill thousands of women and girls. Guns offer already dangerous people an opportunity to brutalize greater numbers of women at one time, says Dahle. She also details the ways in which men use guns to keep already struggling women down. She concludes that women's human rights end up violated when men have easy access to guns.

Dahle is a coordinator for Amnesty International and a women's rights activist who has worked on many campaigns, including the Convention to Eliminate All Forms of Discrimination Against Women.

Today [November 25, 2011] marks the beginning of the annual international 16 Days of Activism Against Gender Violence campaign. Since 1991, over 3,700 organizations in at least 164 countries have participated in the campaign, which runs from

November 25, the International Day Against Violence Against Women, through December 10, International Human Rights Day, to emphasize the connection between violence against women and the violation of women's human rights. . . .

Guns and Violence Against Women

Although the vast majority of those who make, sell, buy, own and use guns are men, large numbers of women and girls are affected directly and indirectly by armed violence in their homes, in their communities and during and after armed conflict.

Women around the world are at greatest risk of gun violence, not on the streets or in combat zones, but in their own homes.

Pakistani women rally against gender violence and discrimination. In the United States women have experienced a 272 percent increase in the risk of gun violence against them in the home.

More than 75% of the nearly 900 million small arms in the world are owned by private individuals—mostly men—and kept in their homes. A gun in a home is much more likely to be used to intimidate or injure a family member than to be used against an intruder. Family killings are the only type of homicide where women outnumber men as victims. Guns are the weapons of choice in domestic violence, and when a woman is killed in her home, her partner or a male relative is most likely to be the murderer. According to research in the USA, just having a gun in the house increases the risk of someone in the home being murdered by 41%, but for women in particular, the risk is nearly tripled with an increase of 272%.

Guns Are Used to Intimidate, Rape, and Kill

Women also encounter gun violence in the community outside their homes at the hands of police, immigration and security officers, border guards, military and paramilitary personnel and criminal gangs. Both security officials and armed criminals can use their guns to threaten, intimidate, rape or kill women and girls, especially in areas where law enforcement officers are poorly trained and equipped, where those responsible for gun violence are not brought to justice, and where there is a widespread lack of respect for the human rights of women. When armed gangs are active in a community, women may fear going to work collecting water or firewood and going about their daily lives. In places where the criminal justice system is weak, corrupt, or simply does not take violence against women seriously, women are often afraid to even report violent abuse for fear of shaming their families or retribution from the perpetrators.

Because of easy access to small arms of all kinds, modern conflicts frequently target civilians for war crimes, crimes against humanity, and mass rape as a weapon of war. As Annie Matundu Mbambi of the Democratic Republic of Congo said in a recent interview, "A guy with a machete in a village can rape one woman. Two guys with a machine gun can rape the whole village." Such violent conflict forces women to flee, leaving their

Women More Likely to Feel Less Safe Around Guns

Women are more likely to feel less comfortable with allowing people to carry guns openly in public, according to data from the Brady Center to Prevent Gun Violence.

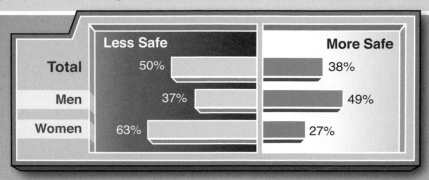

	Less Safe	More Safe
Total	50%	38%
Men	37%	49%
Women	63%	27%

Older women, along with racial and ethnic minority women and women in urban areas, are the strongest in their opposition to policies that let people carry guns openly.

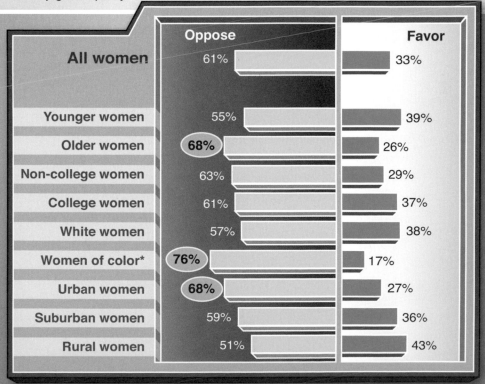

	Oppose	Favor
All women	61%	33%
Younger women	55%	39%
Older women	68%	26%
Non-college women	63%	29%
College women	61%	37%
White women	57%	38%
Women of color*	76%	17%
Urban women	68%	27%
Suburban women	59%	36%
Rural women	51%	43%

*Includes all women who are not white.

Figures do not total 100 percent because some participants answered "unsure."

Taken from: Brady Center to Prevent Gun Violence, "Findings from a National Survey of 600 Registered Voters," April 25–28, 2010.

homes, livelihoods and communities behind. Women are forced to become heads of their households caring for their children, the elderly and those with disabilities single handedly when their male relatives are involved in fighting, or when they are detained, injured or killed. Those who become war widows may lose their land, family support, and status in the community.

Guns Make Horrible Crimes Even Worse

Even when armed conflict is officially over, the brutalizing effects of war do not end. When combatants return to their communities, many bring the trauma and violence of the fighting into their homes. If men bring their weapons home with them, the women and girls who live with them are at high risk for threatening and violent treatment.

To reduce the availability of guns used to commit violence against women around the world, the Arms Trade Treaty currently under negotiation at the United Nations should require countries to prevent any international transfer of conventional arms when there is a substantial risk the arms are likely to be used to commit serious violations of international human rights law or international humanitarian law. Such regulations could help ensure that human rights offenders—particularly, those who use small arms to commit egregious acts of violence against women—do not get their hands on the instruments of violence and repression. As the negotiations move forward, we must continue to hold governments responsible for protecting their citizens and upholding the human rights of women who live within their borders.

SEVEN

Gun Violence Particularly Threatens Children

Children's Defense Fund

In the following viewpoint, the advocacy group Children's Defense Fund argues that children are particularly threatened by gun violence. They report that guns have killed more than one hundred thousand children since 1979. Each year, a child is killed by a gun every three hours. According to the Children's Defense Fund, children are not safe in their own homes; they find or steal guns from their parents and use them to kill themselves or to shoot their friends, either by accident or on purpose. Children are also not safe at school; a significant percentage of high school students have carried a weapon, and many of them have brought a gun to school. Some students stay home from school because they feel so unsafe. The authors say that guns have killed more children than the number of soldiers killed in the Vietnam, Iraq, and Afghanistan wars combined. They conclude that America's children deserve to be safe from gun violence, whether at home, at school, or in their neighborhoods.

The Children's Defense Fund seeks to improve and establish programs and policies that benefit, protect, and service children.

We [the Children's Defense Fund] dedicate this 12th child gun death report to the memory of Trayvon Martin[1] and the thousands of children and teenagers killed by guns each year in America. As we publish on March 23, 2012, to demand justice for Trayvon, hundreds of thousands of people across the country have poured into the streets—from New York to Sanford, Florida—to demand justice for Trayvon. Hundreds of thousands more stepped up to protest online. In response to the public outcry, the Sanford Chief of Police has temporarily stepped down and the state prosecutor has stepped aside. But nearly one month after 17-year-old Trayvon Martin was stopped, stalked, shot and killed while walking home from a convenience store, armed only with a bag of Skittles and a can of iced tea, his killer, George Zimmerman, has not been arrested.

The public outrage over Trayvon's tragic death is right and just, and we hope it will be sustained until justice is done. But where is the outrage over every single one of the thousands of children and teens killed by guns every year in our nation—too many killed by gun-toting Americans unrestrained by common sense gun control laws? Florida's "Stand Your Ground" law, also known as the "shoot first, ask questions later" law, is now under national scrutiny. But will it and other laws be changed to protect children rather than gun owners and gun sellers? What is it going to take to get the American public and leaders to stand up to protect the lives and safety of children first?

Children and Teens Are Not Safe

Next month, April 16th [2012], marks the fifth anniversary of the Virginia Tech massacre in which 32 students and faculty were killed by a gun, 25 others were injured, and many more were traumatized. Each year since then has seen shootings with multiple victims—young children, teenagers, young adults, a Member of Congress, a federal judge and many more. Days, weeks, months

1. An unarmed teen who was shot and killed in Sanford, Florida, by volunteer neighborhood watchman George Zimmerman in February 2012.

and years go by and little or nothing—except fleeting headlines, tears, trauma and talk—is done to protect children.

- A total of 5,740 children and teens died in 2008 and 2009, the two years after the Virginia Tech shooting, according to the most recent data from the federal Centers for Disease Control and Prevention. This is the equivalent of one child or teen being killed by a gun every three hours, or eight each day over those two years, or 229 public school classrooms with 25 students each.

Police investigate the scene in Brockton, Massachusetts, where a fifteen-year-old boy was shot and killed in 2003.

- Gun homicide continued as the leading cause of death among black teens 15 to 19. White teens the same age were more likely to die from motor vehicle accidents, followed by gun homicide in 2008 and gun suicide in 2009.
- Black males 15 to 19 were eight times as likely as white males the same age and two-and-a-half-times as likely as their Hispanic peers to be gun homicide victims in 2009.
- Non-fatal gun injuries and the physical and emotional trauma that follows afflicted 34,387 children and teens over two years, 20,596 in 2008 and 13,791 in 2009.
- Taking a 30-year snapshot when child gun death and injury data collection began, 116,385 children and teens were killed by firearms between 1979 and 2009—enough to fill 4,655 public school classrooms of 25 students each. Since 1979, America has lost nearly three times as many children and teens to gunfire as the number of U.S. military personnel killed in action during the Vietnam War, and over 23 times the number of U.S. military personnel killed in action in Iraq and Afghanistan (5,013).

American Children Are Under Assault

Where is our anti-war movement here at home? Why does a nation with the largest military budget in the world refuse to protect its children from relentless gun violence and terrorism at home? No external enemy ever killed thousands of children in their neighborhoods, streets and schools year in and year out. By any standards of human and moral decency, children in America are under assault, and by international standards, America remains an unparalleled world leader in gun deaths of children and teens—a distinction we shamefully and immorally choose! *The most recent analysis of data from 23 high-income countries reported that 87 percent of children under age 15 killed by guns in these nations lived in the United States. And the U.S. gun homicide rate for teens and young adults 15 to 24 was 42.7 times higher than the combined gun homicide rate for that same age group in the other countries.*

Common-Sense Gun Laws Are Needed

Why are common-sense gun regulations so shockingly absent in our country? Even in the wake of the tragedy in Tucson[2] and the near-fatal shooting of one of their own, Congress failed to take action. Calls for banning high-volume ammunition clips and tightening up the federal background check system were ignored. Instead, our leaders once again answered the call of gun owners and the powerful gun lobby over the rights of children and citizens to life and safety. In November 2011, the U.S. House of Representatives passed the National Right-to-Carry Reciprocity Act. If a similar bill is passed by the Senate and becomes law, a person with a permit to carry a concealed handgun in one state—a person like George Zimmerman in Sanford, Florida—could carry that concealed weapon in another state even if it was against that second state's law. Proponents of such ill-conceived gun trafficking laws maintain the fiction that guns promote personal safety.

Our leaders in Washington, D.C. are not alone in refusing to make America safer for children. Forty-two states have adopted preemption laws to ensure that state legislatures have control of gun policy, impeding the ability of cities to develop local solutions to gun violence in their communities suggesting that they know best although states continue to make decisions detrimental to children. In 2011, Kansas, Mississippi and Utah enacted laws allowing concealed weapon permit holders to carry loaded, concealed firearms in or on the grounds of elementary and secondary schools. With all eyes on Florida's "Stand Your Ground" law, few noticed a law passed last year that, if upheld, threatens loss of a medical license for doctors who ask patients about whether a gun is in the home although it is not at all unusual and completely sensible for pediatricians particularly to ask patients and parents of patients about possible safety hazards in the home, including guns.

We have so much work to do to build safe communities and a safe nation for our children. We need leaders at all levels of

2. The 2011 shooting in Arizona by Jared Lee Loughner that resulted in six deaths and thirteen wounded, including Congresswoman Gabrielle Giffords.

government who will protect children rather than guns and we need a relentless, powerful citizens' voice to break the gun lobby's veto on sane gun policy. Our laws must control who can obtain firearms and close the gun show loophole, require consumer safety standards and childproof safety features for all firearms, and strengthen child access prevention laws that ensure guns in the home are stored safely and securely. We *all* must take action. We *all* must ask candidates this fall what steps they will take to protect children from guns.

The Sanctity of Life

We must remove guns from our homes where children so often find them and put themselves and others in harm's way. We must teach our children nonviolent ways to resolve conflicts and we must reject pervasive violence in our culture—on TV programs, songs, in movies, and on the Internet. And we must engage our young people in purposeful activities that will keep them away from gangs, drugs, violence, and guns.

As a nation, we must step down from our role as world leader in child gun deaths and work together to make America a moral leader in protecting children in the world which must begin with *preventing* and *reducing* gun deaths of children and teens and of all who reside here. Every child's life is sacred and it is long past time that we protect it. The greatest national security threat in America comes from no enemy without but from armed enemies within who lack regard for the sanctity of life for every vulnerable child. . . .

Child and Teen Gun Deaths

5,740 children and teens died from gunfire in the United States in 2008 and 2009.

- 2,947 children and teens were killed by guns in 2008; another 2,793 were killed in 2009. Two-thirds were victims of homicide (3,892), one-quarter were suicides (1,548), and five percent were accidental or unknown (300) gun deaths.

Firearm Deaths of Children and Teens, 2007
United States Total: 3,042

WA 32
OR 15
ID 14
MT 8
ND 3
MN 27
NH 1
VT 2
ME 5
NY 107
MA 31
RI 0
WY 6
SD 5
WI 57
MI 119
PA 126
CT 14
NV 38
NE 20
IA 15
IL 150
IN 50
OH 104
WV 10
VA 76
NJ 53
DE 7
UT 15
CO 33
KS 36
MO 85
KY 42
MD 82
CA 431
NC 91
DC 26
AZ 82
NM 36
OK 45
AR 35
TN 61
SC 60
MS 50
AL 69
GA 114
TX 250
LA 114
FL 176
AK 14
HI 0

Taken from: US Department of Health and Human Services, Centers for Disease Control and Prevention, National Center for Injury Prevention and Control, WISQARS, *Protect Children, Not Guns*. www.cdc.gov/ncipc/wisqars. Calculations by Children's Defense Fund, 2010.

Black children and teens were only 15 percent of the child population but were 45 percent of the total fatal gun deaths in 2008 and 2009.

• Overall, gun deaths among children and teens declined slightly (three percent) between 2007 and 2008, and declined an additional five percent between 2008 and 2009.

  • *Between 2008 and 2009*, 154 fewer children and teens died from guns. There were 182 fewer homicides, nine fewer accidental gun deaths, and 15 fewer gun deaths classified as unknown. Suicides with a gun increased by 52 offsetting the overall decline in gun deaths.

- *Between 2007 and 2008,* 95 fewer children and teens died from guns. Although 160 fewer children and teens died in homicide, accidental and unknown gun deaths (124, 15 and 21 fewer deaths respectively), the increase of 65 suicide deaths offset the overall decline in gun deaths.
- The number of children and teens killed by guns in 2008 and 2009 would fill more than 229 public school classrooms of 25 students each.
- The number of *preschoolers* killed by guns in 2008 (88) and 2009 (85) was nearly double the number of law enforcement officers killed in the line of duty in 2008 (41) and 2009 (48).
- Sixty-six percent of the gun deaths of children and teens in 2009 were homicides; 29 percent were suicides. Among adults the trend is the opposite: 34 percent of gun deaths in 2009 were homicides and 64 percent were suicides.
- Eighty-seven percent of children and teens killed by guns in 2009 were boys (2,434). Boys ages 15 to 19 were more than seven times as likely as girls that age to commit suicide with a gun.
- Eighty-seven percent of gun deaths of children and teens in 2009 occurred among teens ages 15 to 19 years old. In fact, more 15 to 19 year olds died from gunshot wounds in 2009 than from any other cause except motor vehicle accidents.
- Between 1979 and 2009 gun deaths among white children and teens have *decreased* by 44 percent, compared to an overall 30 percent *increase* among black children and teens over the same period.
- Ninety percent of gun deaths of black children and teens in 2009 were homicides (1,092); six percent were suicides (72). Among white children and teens, almost half of all gun deaths in 2009 were homicides (730) while 46 percent were suicides (698). White children and teens are twice as likely to commit suicide by gun as black children and teens.
- In 2009, 43 percent of gun deaths were black children and teens and 54 percent were white; 59 percent of homicide victims were black children and teens; 87 percent of suicide victims were white. . . .

116,385 children and teens in America have died from gun violence in the 30 years since 1979.

- The number of children and teens killed by guns since 1979 would fill 4,655 public school classrooms of 25 students each or Boston's Fenway Park [major league baseball stadium] three times over.
- Since 1979, America has lost nearly three times as many children and teens to gunfire as the number of U.S. military deaths during the Vietnam War and over 23 times the number of U.S. military deaths in Iraq and Afghanistan.
- Of the 116,385 children killed by guns since 1979, 59 percent were white and 38 percent were black.
- The majority of gun deaths among children since 1979 have been homicides (57 percent) while nearly one-third have been suicides (31 percent).
- The number of black children and teens killed by gunfire in the 30 years since 1979 is nearly 13 times greater than the number of recorded lynchings of black people of all ages in America in the 86 years between 1882 and 1968.

EIGHT

Widespread Gun Ownership Puts Police at Risk

Brady Center to Prevent Gun Violence

In the following viewpoint, the Brady Center to Prevent Gun Violence argues that guns threaten law enforcement officers. Because many gun laws are weak and ineffective, it says, many guns end up in criminals' hands, which makes police work infinitely more dangerous than it already is. Armed criminals increase the chances that police officers will get injured or killed when they make traffic stops, enter residences, or respond to distress calls. According to the Brady Center, a law enforcement officer dies each week, on average, as a result of a heavily armed criminal contingent. The Brady Center says that law enforcement is by its nature a dangerous job, but it is made more dangerous when criminals can get numerous, powerful guns easily.

The Brady Center to Prevent Gun Violence is a leading national advocate for gun control and has sponsored numerous laws intended to curb gun violence and minimize the risk guns pose to children, neighborhoods, and police officers.

Officer Jillian Smith was shot and killed while shielding an 11-year-old girl from gunfire. Sergeant Timothy Prunty was shot to death in an ambush as he stood next to his patrol car outside a convenience store. Officer Matthew Tokuoka and Sergeant Anthony Wallace were shot and killed in front of their families by a man both officers had previously arrested. Special

Police officers bear the coffin of a fallen comrade. The author argues that weak gun laws and an ever-increasing number of civilian gun owners put police at high risk of injury and death.

Agent Jaime Zapata was forced off the road and shot to death in Mexico. Officer John Falcone was shot and killed on a downtown street by a man who had just killed his [own] wife and who then killed himself.

An Officer Dies Every Week

These are just a few of the deadly incidents of gun violence against law enforcement officers in recent years. Since 2009, at least 122 law enforcement officers have been shot and killed, with an average of one officer shot and killed every week during that time.

Fatal shootings in the line of duty are increasing. 2010 saw a 24% increase in officer deaths by gunfire over the previous year, and 2011 is on track to be even bloodier.

Since the beginning of 2011 [to May 2011], there have been at least thirty officer deaths by gunfire. . . .

Weak Gun Laws Endanger Officers' Lives

It is far too easy for dangerous people to obtain guns in America as a result of loopholes in federal gun laws and weak—often nonexistent—state gun laws.

Weak gun laws: 1) allow the easy availability of assault weapons and assault clips, which have been used against law enforcement officers with increasing frequency since the federal Assault Weapons Ban expired in 2004; 2) allow dangerous people to buy firearms at gun shows without Brady background checks[1]; and 3) place severe constraints on law enforcement that allow corrupt gun dealers to fuel the criminal gun market without punishment. . . .

Weak gun laws that arm criminals in the United States are also arming Mexican drug trafficking organizations, with disastrous consequences for law enforcement officers in Mexico and in the U.S.

1. Submitting background checks for would-be gun buyers is part of the Brady Handgun Violence Prevention Act of 1993, named after James Brady, former press secretary to President Ronald Reagan, who was shot and partially paralyzed during a 1981 attempt to assassinate the president.

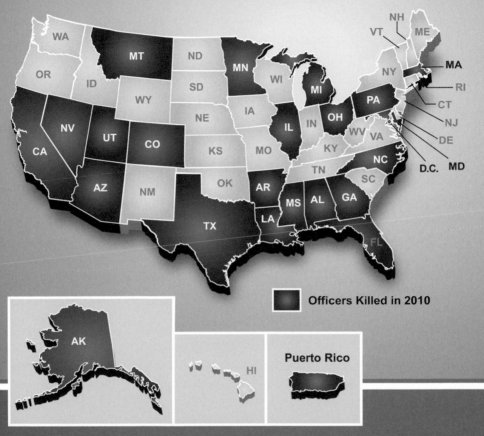

A total of 56 officers in 22 states and Puerto Rico were killed in the line of duty during 2010.

Officers Killed in 2010

Taken from: Federal Bureau of Investigation, "In the Line of Duty: 56 Officers Feloniously Killed in 2010," October 24, 2011. www.fbi.gov/news/stories/2011/october/leoka_10211/leoka_102411.

In 2011, we saw the first gun death of a U.S. agent in Mexico since 1985. We have also seen recent shootings of U.S. law enforcement agents with straw purchased and trafficked guns [bought by someone to give or sell to someone else] bought in this country that were meant to arm Mexican drug trafficking organizations.

Police Officers Need Protection

We need common-sense gun laws that make it harder for dangerous people to get deadly weapons. Policy solutions to help reduce the bloodshed against law enforcement and our communities include:

- Banning the sale of assault weapons and assault clips that turn firearms into weapons of war
- Closing the gun show loophole that allows gun sales without background checks to dangerous criminals
- Enacting one handgun per month restrictions that limit bulk sales of handguns to straw buyers and gun traffickers
- Strengthening federal law to allow felony prosecutions of gun dealers who knowingly sell to straw purchasers buying guns for traffickers
- Repealing gun industry protections that make it harder for law enforcement to do their jobs by protecting corrupt gun sellers, including repealing the so-called Protection of Lawful Commerce in Arms Act [2005] that shields gun dealers from civil liability for supplying criminals with guns and repealing the Tiahrt Amendments that hinder the Bureau of Alcohol, Tobacco, Firearms and Explosives' (ATF's) ability to inspect, sanction, or shut down rogue gun dealers.

NINE

Civilian Gun Ownership Helps Police Fight Crime

John Stossel

In the following viewpoint, John Stossel argues that when civilians own guns, they can help police fight crime. He details several situations in which armed civilians were able to hold off a gunman until police arrived on the scene. Even when people are not able to directly stop a gunman, says Stossel, criminals will be less likely to act if they suspect the people they intend to criminalize have guns, too. In his opinion, an armed population that is willing and able to defend itself relieves some of the pressure on the police force. He concludes that Americans should not rely on the police or government to protect them and that if everyone participated in self-defense, society would be much safer.

Formerly coanchor of the ABC News program *20/20*, Stossel currently appears in his own show on the Fox Business channel. He is also the author of the book *Myths, Lies, and Downright Stupidity*.

It's all too predictable. A day after a gunman killed six people and wounded 18 others at Northern Illinois University, the *New York Times* criticized the U.S. Interior Department for preparing to rethink its ban on guns in national parks.

The editorial board wants "the 51 senators who like the thought of guns in the parks—and everywhere else, it seems—to realize that the innocence of Americans is better protected by carefully controlling guns than it is by arming everyone to the teeth."

Criminals Do Not Care About the Law

As usual, the *Times* editors seem unaware of how silly their argument is. To them, the choice is between "carefully controlling guns" and "arming everyone to the teeth." But no one favors "arming everyone to the teeth" (whatever that means). Instead, gun advocates favor freedom, choice and self-responsibility. If someone wishes to be prepared to defend himself, he should be free to do so. No one has the right to deprive others of the means of effective self-defense, like a handgun.

As for the first option, "carefully controlling guns," how many shootings at schools or malls will it take before we understand that people who intend to kill are not deterred by gun laws? Last I checked, murder is against the law everywhere. No one intent on murder will be stopped by the prospect of committing a lesser crime like illegal possession of a firearm. The intellectuals and politicians who make pious declarations about controlling guns should explain how their gunless utopia is to be realized. While they search for—excuse me—their magic bullet, innocent people are dying defenseless.

Gun-Free Zones Are Havens for Crime

That's because laws that make it difficult or impossible to carry a concealed handgun do deter one group of people: law-abiding citizens who might have used a gun to stop crime. Gun laws are laws against self-defense. Criminals have the initiative. They choose the time, place and manner of their crimes, and they tend to make choices that maximize their own, not their victims', success. So criminals don't attack people they know are armed, and anyone thinking of committing mass murder is likely to be attracted to a gun-free zone, such as schools and malls.

"We can't rob this bank. They won't let us bring these guns inside!"

Cartoon © 2008 by Chaim Cartoons. Reproduced by permission.

Self-Defense Is the Best Defense

Government may promise to protect us from criminals, but it cannot deliver on that promise. This was neatly summed up in book title a few years ago, *Dial 911 and Die*. If you are the target of a crime, only one other person besides the criminal is sure to be on the scene: you. There is no good substitute for self-responsibility.

How, then, does it make sense to create mandatory gun-free zones, which in reality are free-crime zones?

The usual suspects keep calling for more gun control laws. But this idea that gun control is crime control is just a myth. The National Academy of Sciences reviewed dozens of studies and could not find a single gun regulation that clearly led to reduced violent crime or murder. When Washington, D.C., passed its tough handgun ban years ago, gun violence rose.

Armed Citizens Can Help Police

The press ignores the fact that guns often save lives. It's what happened in 2002 at the Appalachian School of Law. Hearing shots,

In Pearl, Mississippi, school shooter Luke Woodham (center) was stopped when the school's vice principal armed himself with a gun from his truck and ran to the scene. Gun owners say that armed citizens have stopped many violent crimes from occurring.

two students went to their cars, got their guns and restrained the shooter until police arrested him.

Likewise, law professor Glen Reynolds writes, "Pearl, Miss., school shooter Luke Woodham was stopped [on October 1, 1997] when the school's vice principal took a .45 [gun] from his truck and ran to the scene. In February's Utah mall shooting [in 2008], it was an off-duty police officer who happened to be on the scene and carrying a gun [who stopped the shooter]."

It's impossible to know exactly how often guns stop criminals. Would-be victims don't usually report crimes that don't happen. But people use guns in self-defense every day. The Cato Institute's Tom Palmer says just showing his gun to muggers once saved his life.

"It equalizes unequals," Mr. Palmer told [ABC News program] *20/20*. "If someone gets into your house, which would you rather have, a handgun or a telephone? You can call the police if you want, and they'll get there, and they'll take a picture of your dead body. But they can't get there in time to save your life. The first line of defense is you."

TEN

Tighter Gun Control Laws Can Reduce Gun Violence

USA Today

In the following viewpoint, the editors of *USA Today* argue that the right to bear arms comes with a responsibility to restrict their use. They say supporters of gun ownership rights have gone too far in pushing for people to be able to carry guns in public and for getting off the hook should someone kill a person by mistake. In the editors' view, there is little need to bring guns to schools, churches, restaurants, sporting events, and other places where people expect to be able to congregate safely. According to the editors, it is impossible to truly be free when guns are so prevalent in the public sphere. They conclude that the Second Amendment has been too loosely interpreted and that tighter gun control laws are needed to keep people safe.

USA Today is a widely read national daily newspaper.

When it comes to gun fights, things are pretty quiet on the Potomac these days. Democrats, cowed by the National Rifle Association's political clout, have no taste for pushing gun control up the agenda. And even if they did, the landmark 2008 Supreme Court ruling that the Second Amendment provides a right for individuals to own guns largely leaves them disarmed.

From Radical to Idiotic

The states, however, are another matter. Gun rights activists have taken their national victories not as a reason to pat themselves on the back, but as reason to push forward with an agenda that ranges from radical to idiotic.

Last month [March 2011] for instance, Wyoming joined Arizona, Alaska and Vermont to become the fourth state to allow concealed firearms with no permit whatsoever. Also last month,

The viewpoint's authors argue that many states have taken the right to bear arms to a dangerous level. Here, for example, Wisconsin governor Scott Walker (seated) signs into law in July 2011 a bill allowing the state's residents to carry concealed weapons.

Mississippi removed most of the exceptions to its concealed weapons law, allowing people to take guns to sporting events, and into bars, churches, schools and colleges, among other places. Just this month, North Dakota joined more than a dozen other states that have said an employer cannot ban an employee from bringing a weapon to work, so long as it is kept in the worker's vehicle.

Even if you view this as a legitimate exercise of personal freedom, it's hardly wise, or without limitations on the freedom of others. Take the rights of property owners, for instance. Under many of these laws, businesses cannot object to someone bringing a weapon onto their premises.

Guns Cannot Be Accepted Everywhere

Pennsylvania, meanwhile, is on the verge of becoming the latest to join the craze of states passing laws described as "stand your ground" by supporters and "shoot first" by critics. These give people who use deadly force in public places many of the same protections they might have in defending their homes from an intruder. They remove an individual's obligation to retreat from a threatening situation if such an option exists. And in many cases they provide a legal defense should he or she kill or injure an innocent bystander by mistake.

What we are seeing is a systematic campaign for a doctrine of guns anywhere, anytime and in the hands of just about anyone, without consequence for irresponsible actions. When the gun lobby first started winning concealed carry laws about two decades ago, it said that vigorous background checks and permitting procedures should be maintained, and that some places should remain gun-free. Having won such laws in most states, it is now working to undo those parameters.

Confusion About the Second Amendment

The gun lobby is also going after the two states (Wisconsin and Illinois) that do not allow concealed firearms, and the nine that leave the issuance of a permit to the discretion of law enforcement. In [their] one major foray into Congress recently, gun extremists

Comparing Concealed Weapons Laws from 1981 and 2011

The maps below demonstrate how laws regulating the carrying of concealed weapons have changed over 30 years.

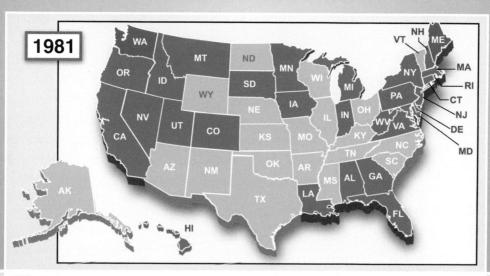

No Carry: Concealed carry is prohibited [1981: 19 states; 2011: 1 state and Washington, DC].

May Issue: Concealed carry is allowed with a permit, and the issuing agency has discretion to grant or deny a permit [1981: 28 states and Washington, DC; 2011: 10 states].

Shall Issue: Concealed carry is allowed with a permit, but the issuing agency has no discretion and must grant a permit to anyone who meets minimum qualifications [1981: 2 states; 2011: 35 states].

No Permit Required: Concealed carry is allowed and no permit is required [1981: 1 state; 2011: 4 states].

Taken from: Legal Community Against Violence, *Guns in Public Places*, July 5, 2011.

fell just two votes shy in the U.S. Senate on a 2009 bill that would have forced any state to recognize a carry permit issued by any other state. That measure—a monumental infringement on states rights and local governance, to say the least—would have forced urbanized states dealing with gangs, drug lords and other violent criminals to essentially adopt gun rights deemed appropriate in more rural states.

These are precisely the kinds of results that opponents of gun rights predicted during the multi-decade debate over the confused meaning of the Second Amendment. From a constitutional perspective, the Supreme Court may have gotten it right. But from a standpoint of public safety, lawmakers are getting it very wrong. A right to keep and bear arms should come with restraints that equally protect those who have no interest in owning them.

ELEVEN

Gun Control Laws Restrict Those Least Likely to Commit Violence

Don B. Kates Jr.

Gun control laws restrict those least likely to commit crimes, argues Don B. Kates Jr. in the following viewpoint. He explains that people who use guns to rob, threaten, and kill are, by their nature, not law-abiding citizens. The vast majority of them are already felons and are, by law, not allowed to own guns. But criminals care little for the laws on the books, says Kates, and will likely disregard all laws made about guns. Therefore, the only people restrained by gun control laws are law-abiding citizens, whom Kates says can play a valuable role in standing up to criminals. He concludes that gun control laws punish law-abiding citizens while having no effect on criminals.

Kates is a criminologist and constitutional lawyer. He is a research fellow with the Independent Institute, a think tank located in Oakland, California.

The March 21 [2009] murder of four Oakland police officers by Lovelle Mixon, a convicted felon wanted for a recent parole violation, epitomizes the futility of "gun control," or the banning and restricting of gun ownership for law-abiding adults. Using the officers' tragic deaths to further an unrelated agenda—stripping away the Second Amendment rights of honorable citizens—is both harmful and distracting.

Law-Abiding People Do Not Commit Crimes

Mixon was not an anomaly. Felons commit over 90 percent of murders, with the remainder carried out primarily by juveniles and the mentally unbalanced. The United States already has laws forbidding all three groups from owning guns, which, by definition, are ineffective against the lawless. "Gun control," therefore, only "controls" those who have done nothing to merit such regulations.

A memorial is held for four Oakland, California, police officers shot to death by paroled felon Lovelle Mixon. Gun control opponents say the incident underscores the fact that criminals do not abide by gun control laws.

Arguments for gun control rest on deceptive claims such as National Coalition to Ban Handguns' allegation that "most murders are committed by previously law-abiding citizens." Americans are deluged by literally dozens of supposedly scholarly articles asserting such falsehoods—but with no supporting references. For there are none.

Notably, only 15 percent of all Americans have criminal records, yet more than 90 percent of murder suspects have a history of crime. Their criminal careers average six or more years' length, including four major adult felonies, in addition to their often extensive juvenile records.

Criminals Disregard Gun Control Laws

A *New York Times* study of the 1,662 murders in that city between 2003 and 2005 found that "more than 90 percent of the killers had criminal records." Baltimore police records show similar statistics for its murder suspects in 2006. In Milwaukee, police reported that most murder suspects in 2007 had criminal records, while "a quarter of them [killed while] on probation or parole." The great majority of Illinois murderers from the years 1991–2000 had prior felony records. Eighty percent of Atlanta murder arrestees had previously been arrested at least once for a drug offense; 70 percent had three or more prior drug arrests—in addition to their arrests for other crimes.

In sum, guns or no guns, neither most murderers nor many murderers—nor virtually any murderers—are ordinary, law-abiding, responsible adults. This conclusion is so invariably reached by homicide studies that the 1998 study by David Kennedy and Anthony Braga describes the fact that murderers are almost invariably veteran criminals as a standard "criminological axiom."

Guns Help Keep the Peace

Naïve, well-meaning people often respond to such facts with, "Still, wouldn't this be a better world without guns?" After many years of studying guns as a highly effective method of self-defense,

I reply, no, the world would be immeasurably worse off without the only weaponry that gives the weak a real chance against predators. After all, there was a time, hundreds of years ago, when there were no guns. Without guns for self-defense, survival was measured by the strength of men's arms, as women, children and the elderly huddled in terror, escaping only by abject submission to their predators. Yes, Mixon used a gun to kill four Oakland police officers. But had he not been shot and killed by another member of the SWAT team, the death toll would have been undoubtedly higher. In the hands of sworn officers and moral citizens, guns are a powerful, swift means of protection. When the government passes laws that only peaceable people obey, they are simply leaving the same people at the mercy of violent predators.

TWELVE

Reinstate Ban on Military-Style Assault Weapons

Arizona Daily Star

> In the following viewpoint, the editors of the *Arizona Daily Star* argue that assault weapons should be banned. They explain that assault weapons are very powerful, deadly weapons that give shooters the ability to pierce armor, shoot from great distances, spray multiple bullets into crowds of people, and even to bring down airplanes and explode fuel tanks. In their opinion, the only purpose of such weapons is to kill large groups of people and cause enormous chaos and destruction. No American should have this need or right, they say. Assault weapons put the general public at risk and leave police at a disadvantage against very well armed criminals. The editors conclude that assault weapons are too deadly to be allowed and exceed the parameters of the Second Amendment.
>
> The *Arizona Daily Star* is a daily newspaper based in Tucson.

This country needs to re-impose a new, effective ban on military-style assault weapons. Banning semiautomatic assault weapons designed to kill lots of people quickly isn't quite as simple as it may appear on the surface. That must not keep us from trying.

In fact, even given myriad defects in the now-expired federal assault-weapons ban, we could do a lot worse than essentially reinstating it as originally written. Flawed though it was, it reduced the flow of such weapons.

Even better, Congress should consider emulating California's assault-weapons ban.

The 1994–2004 federal ban was riddled with loopholes. The law outlawed the sale and possession of 19 specific types of weapons; it also outlawed "copycat" weapons that had two or more combat features—such as bayonet mounts, threads for silencers, pistol grips or flash suppressors. But if you made a copycat without two of the listed combat characteristics, it was legal.

An example, from Charles Heller, secretary of the Arizona Citizens Defense League: AR-15 rifles were banned because, in part, these semiautomatic rifles each weighed more than 50 ounces. But after the ban went into effect, said Heller, gun makers switched from using aluminum to polymer in making AR-15s, thus dropping the weight below 50 ounces and, voila!, the rifles were legal under federal law. Aluminum? Illegal. Polymer? Legal. "The federal ban didn't ban weapons," Heller told us. "It banned cosmetic features on weapons."

A federal ban on assault weapons has been supported by most Americans, including gun owners, in polls conducted over many years. Law enforcement groups also supported the now-expired ban and supported its extensions; among these were the Fraternal Organization of Police, the National Association of Police Organizations, and the National Sheriffs' Association. When criminals are toting military-grade firepower, police are at greater risk—and need comparable weapons to combat the bad guys.

Studies show the expired federal ban did slow the flow of military-style assault weapons in this country. The Brady Campaign to Prevent Gun Violence found in 2004 that 45 percent fewer assault weapons were traced as crime guns by the federal Bureau of Alcohol, Tobacco, Firearms and Explosives while the federal ban was in effect.

Ban on Assault Weapons Worked

According to data compiled by the *Washington Post* during the federal assault weapons ban in place between 1994 and 2004, there was a drop in the percentage of firearms—specifically, those having high-capacity magazines—that were seized by police in Virginia. When the ban expired, the percentage rebounded.

Federal Ban on Assault Weapons, 1994 to 2004

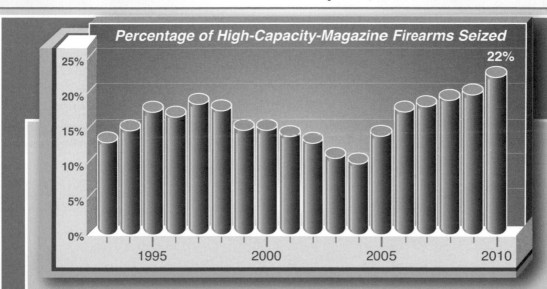

Taken from: David S. Fallis and James V. Grimaldi, "Va. Data Show Drop in Criminal Firepower During Assault Gun Ban," *Washington Post*, January 22, 2011.

The National Rifle Association disagrees with virtually all of this. Key points its Institute for Legislative Action website cites include that such a ban infringes on the right to defense and that it bars weapons that are "functionally identical to millions of other guns."

We believe an imperfect ban is better than none when it comes to assault-style weaponry on our streets.

Accompanied by Los Angeles sheriff Lee Baca (right), US senator Barbara Boxer addresses reporters about her support for a new federal ban on assault weapons (foreground). Most law enforcement officials support such a ban, the author says.

Consider what's at stake: In "The Politics of Gun Control," Robert J. Spitzer pointed out in 2008 that the Barrett .50-caliber sniper rifle is easier to buy legally in most states than a handgun. "Weighing about 28 pounds, this weapon is highly accurate from more than a mile away, and it must be fired while resting on a bipod," Spitzer writes. In 1995 the Rand Corp. observed that the weapon "has the capability of piercing reinforced armor used to protect airplanes, fuel tanks, toxic chemicals, and ground facilities," Spitzer notes.

This country must enact a new federal ban on military-style assault weapons. The Brady Campaign argues that a new federal ban should be modeled on California's law, which uses a "one-feature" test to define outlawed weapons. Thus those with just one military-style feature are illegal. The U.S. essentially outlawed machine guns in 1934. It's time we took similar action against their very lethal descendants.

THIRTEEN

Assault Weapons Should Not Be Banned

Jacob Hornberger

The government should not ban assault weapons, argues Jacob Hornberger in the following viewpoint. He says that in the past, assault weapons bans have been ineffective. They were difficult to enforce and did not prohibit all such weapons but only certain models of the guns. Like many gun rights advocates, Hornberger argues that banning any type of gun, including assault weapons, has little effect on criminals, who tend not to follow laws anyway. More likely, such bans only serve to disarm law-abiding citizens, the very people whom Hornberger says can protect the general populace from criminals. He concludes that even though assault weapons are unpopular, they should not be banned—laws must be based on the Constitution, not on public opinion, he maintains.

Hornberger is founder and president of the Future of Freedom Foundation, a nonprofit advocacy group that promotes social and economic policies that advance individual liberty, the free market, privacy, and small government. He writes regularly for *Freedom Daily*, which is published by the foundation.

Jacob Hornberger, "More Gun Control Nonsense," *Hornberger's Blog,* Future of Freedom Foundation, January 18, 2010. www.fff.org/blog/jghblog2010-01-18.asp. Copyright © 2010 by the Future of Freedom Foundation. All rights reserved. Reproduced by permission.

The *New York Times* has another silly editorial on gun control. The paper's editorial board is calling for a renewal of the assault-weapons ban, which expired in 2004. The paper's justification? "A survey of more than 130 local police chiefs and officials found 37 percent reporting an increase in assault weapons in street crime," along with other evidence indicating an increased criminal use of assault weapons.

Notice the implication: If the Congress reenacts the assault-weapons ban, those violent criminals will obey the law.

Criminals Disregard Laws

Now, if that's not silly, what is? What the *Times* is suggesting is that if Congress makes it illegal to own an assault weapon, the violent criminal will say to himself: "Oh my gosh, it's now illegal to own an assault weapon. I now need to figure out how I am going to commit my robbery or murder without violating the new gun-control law."

That's ridiculous. If a would-be murderer or robber doesn't give a hoot for laws against murder or robbery, why in the world would he give a hoot about a law against owning a gun?

The *Washington Post* recently carried a news article that detailed a big sting operation in Washington, D.C., which is notorious for its gun-control laws. D.C. cops and federal officers set up a phony storefront in which they purchased guns from dozens of people, who were then arrested. The operation also netted $1.5 million of heroin, cocaine, and other illegal drugs. Now, the reason those people were arrested and charged is because they were violating D.C.'s gun-control laws (and drug laws).

But wait a minute! If it's illegal to own guns (and drugs) in D.C. then that should mean that there should be no guns (and drugs) in D.C. right? Isn't that what the *Times*' editorial board is suggesting with its call to renew the assault-weapons ban—that once it is renewed, violent criminals will have respect for the law and decline to violate it?

Bans Are Ineffective

Moreover, what the *Times*' editorial board is perhaps unaware of is that the 2004 assault-weapons ban didn't really ban assault

Americans Do Not Want Assault Weapons Banned

In 2011, for the first time, the Gallup polling organization found greater opposition to than support for a ban on semiautomatic guns or assault rifles.

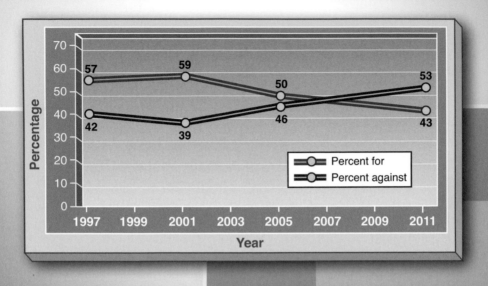

Taken from: Gallup Organization, October 26, 2011.

weapons. It simply banned certain modifications of them, such as extra-long magazines or bayonet holders. It was still possible to acquire the same semi-automatic assault rifles that one can acquire today.

So, what effect would a renewal of the assault-weapons ban have on the ability of violent criminals to get their hands on assault weapons? Alas, the *Times'* editorial board doesn't explain that one.

Do Not Disarm Noncriminals

What is the actual impact of gun control? It disarms noncriminal people, those who don't want to risk a felony conviction for illegally owning the weapon, thereby impeding their ability to defend themselves from criminal-types who have no reservations about violating the gun-control law.

While the *Times* referred to an increased use of assault weapons in "street crime," the title of the *Post*'s article—"In the Market for Guns, Drugs and Arrests," fills in the details: The increase in firepower among violent criminals is undoubtedly part of the infamous war on drugs.

Assault Weapons Flourish Despite Bans

Consider, Mexico, for example, where drug cartels have been employing assault weapons against the cops, the military, rival cartels, and innocent people. No doubt the *Times* would say, "Mexico should make it illegal to own an assault weapon, and that will cure the problem."

A vendor holds an AK-47 assault rifle for sale at a Virginia gun show. Opponents of the assault weapons ban say it will not keep assault rifles out of criminals' hands.

Well, except for one thing: AK-47 assault weapons *are* illegal in Mexico and they are the favored weapon of Mexican drug cartels. In other words, the drug cartels, which have no respect for drug laws and murder laws, have had no respect for Mexico's gun-control law. That must shock the *New York Times*.

The solution to the increase in violence in "street crime" is not gun control but rather drug legalization. Unfortunately, establishment newspapers such as the *New York Times* can't bring themselves to embrace such an obvious libertarian solution. Instead, with hope springing eternal that the 35-year-old drug war can still be won, the *Times* embraces another status intervention, gun control.

Laws Must Be Based on the Constitution

Finally, the *Times* argues that Congress should enact more "realistic gun controls" because polls show the public wants them. I wonder if the *Times* would argue for more realistic "speech controls" if polls show the public wanted them. Unfortunately, the *Times* fails to recognize that fundamental rights are not subject to majority whims, a point that our ancestors understood when they enacted the Bill of Rights.

FOURTEEN

People Should Be Allowed to Carry Guns in Bars

Washington Times

In the following viewpoint, the editors of the *Washington Times* argue that people should be allowed to carry guns in bars and restaurants that serve alcohol. They offer statistics from Virginia showing that when gun owners were allowed to bring their weapons into bars and restaurants, a drop in crime ensued. Furthermore, the editors say, letting people carry weapons while around alcohol had no negative effect, as opponents had claimed it would. The editors conclude that gun owners tend to be law-abiding citizens, and letting them be armed in bars and restaurants intimidates people who are thinking about breaking the law in those establishments.

The *Washington Times* is a conservative daily newspaper in Washington, DC.

Whether it's the economy or gun control, liberals rarely consider the consequences of their misguided schemes. President [Barack] Obama wants more "investment" spending to help the economy even though his nearly $1 trillion in supposed stimulus did nothing to reduce unemployment. Keynesian economics [after English economist John Maynard Keynes, which argues for a significant role of government in the economy] didn't work under [Presidents] Franklin D. Roosevelt or Jimmy Carter, either, but the left refuses to learn the lesson. Now we know that gun-grabber complaints about concealed-carry [laws] in bars and restaurants are nonsense too.

Letting Guns in Bars Reduced Crime

Earlier this month [August 2011], the *Richmond Times-Dispatch* reviewed Virginia State Police records and found the number of firearms-related crimes committed in establishments that serve alcohol dropped 5 percent a year after concealed-carry permit holders could legally pack heat while out on the town. There were 145 gun crimes reported in taverns and eateries a year after the law took effect, compared with 153 before. The *Times-Dispatch* could only identify a single permit holder who had misbehaved, though gun charges later were dropped against that person.

This shouldn't be a surprise to anyone. Gun owners tend to be law-abiding members of their communities. Allowing concealed-carry at the local watering hole did nothing to change that. The Virginia Association of Chiefs of Police worked overtime to defeat restaurant carry, urging Republican Gov. Bob McDonnell to veto the bill in March of last year. "Allowing guns in bars is a recipe for disaster," Virginia Beach Police Chief Jake Jacocks Jr. wrote. "We can fully expect that at some point in the future, a disagreement that today would likely end up in a verbal confrontation, or a bar fight, will inevitably end with gunfire if you sign this legislation into law." The shootouts never happened.

Expanded Gun Rights Keep All Safe

Chief Jacocks said in his letter that he didn't presume to interpret the Second Amendment but that he knew it would be irresponsible to allow "anyone other than a law enforcement officer" to carry a handgun in a bar. Allowing people other than police to protect themselves with firearms is exactly what the right to keep and bear arms is all about. When Mr. Obama took office, the public flocked to gun stores, fearing the imposition of new gun-control measures. Despite the unprecedented number of new gun

Guns in Bars: By State

It is illegal in just eight states to take a loaded gun into a bar or a restaurant that serves alcohol. The majority of states either allow guns in bars or do not specifically prohibit them.

- States that prohibit loaded guns in establishments that serve alcohol.
- States with provisions to allow loaded guns in bars or in other areas of restaurants that serve alcohol.
- States that do not have laws specifically allowing or prohibiting guns in bars or restaurants. (Often these states rely on municipal public nuisance laws.)

Taken from: *New York Times*, "Having a Beer, and Carrying a Weapon," October 4, 2010, and the Legal Community Against Violence.

owners, FBI crime statistics showed violent crime decreased 5.5 percent nationwide between 2010 and 2009. In Virginia's major cities, the drop was 9 percent.

The arguments of the gun-control crowd are like an annoying barfly that needs to be sent home. Expanding the rights of lawful gun owners makes everyone safer.

FIFTEEN

People Should Not Be Allowed to Carry Guns in Bars

Toledo Blade

> The editorial board at the *Toledo Blade* argues in the following viewpoint that it is too dangerous to allow people to bring guns into bars and other places that serve alcohol. They argue that gun rights supporters are wrong when they claim that law-abiding gun owners can be trusted to have guns in bars. The editors suggest that people are law-abiding, until they decide to break the law and offer several instances in which people with no criminal past brought guns to bars, and after having a few drinks, acted irresponsibly and dangerously. They complain that lawmakers—who have allowed guns to be brought to parks, bars, and other public places but not to government offices—are hypocritical on the issue, caring more for their own safety than the safety of the general public. They conclude that mixing guns and alcohol is a bad idea.
>
> The *Toledo Blade* is a daily newspaper in Toledo, Ohio.

If Ohioans are safer when more people carry guns—even in bars—then why are firearms banned in the Statehouse, including the bar that just opened there? And why will guns soon be banned from the Statehouse grounds as well?

When the gun lobby demanded that concealed-carry permit holders be allowed to pack heat wherever they go, Republicans in the General Assembly answered the call to arms by making it legal to bring concealed weapons to parks, sports and concert arenas, restaurants, bars, and other public places. The pro-gun argument was that law-abiding permit holders are no threat to anyone. Indeed, they said, everyone would be safer because the bad guys would not know who might be armed. Yet lawmakers did not extend that level of supposed safety to themselves. Instead, they bravely banned legally licensed guns from the Statehouse and its underground garage, leaving themselves at the mercy of armed criminals.

Doublespeak on Guns

The Capitol Square Review and Advisory Board wants to go further. Last week, it voted to prohibit concealed weapons from the grounds around the Statehouse as well. Advisory board members

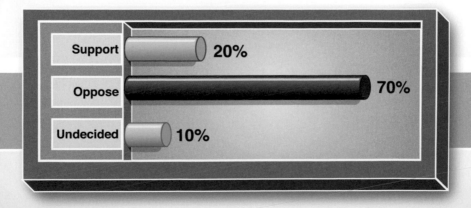

Guns and Alcohol

In 2010 Tennessee enacted a law which allows those with handgun carry permits to take their weapons into establishments that sell alcohol. The majority of Tennesseans opposed the law.

Support 20%

Oppose 70%

Undecided 10%

Taken from: Mason & Dixon Polling Research, Inc., *Tennessean*, July 28, 2010.

told the *Columbus Dispatch* that the prohibition would ensure that the property surrounding the Statehouse "continues to be a safe gathering place."

So which is it? If guns make you safer, why aren't they allowed in the legislature's workplace, parking garage, or semiprivate bar? If an armed society is a civil society, why does the advisory board believe that no guns is a better policy? Self-evidently, lawmakers who voted to allow concealed guns in bars valued their own safety—and the favor of the gun lobby—more than they valued public safety.

Guns and Alcohol Are a Dangerous Mix

But the people who believe that only bad guys break the law have taken a couple of hits recently. This month, Tennessee state Rep. Curry Todd, a Republican from suburban Memphis who sponsored

Although carrying concealed weapons is now legal in Tennessee, many communities in the state have decided, nonetheless, not to allow guns in bars.

his state's concealed-carry law, was arrested for driving under the influence and having a licensed—and loaded—handgun stowed between the front seats of his vehicle. He was stopped by police for driving 60 mph in a 40 mph zone.

The next day, a gun-permit holder from the Cincinnati area reportedly had a couple of beers at a Deer Park bar and got into an argument with another patron. According to police, he left the bar but returned with a pistol, which he brandished as he threatened to kill the man he had argued with. He was arrested.

People Are Law-Abiding—Until They Are Not

These incidents show that not just criminals do stupid things when guns and alcohol are mixed. Even law-abiding people make bad choices, and alcohol can further impair already faulty judgment. Lawmakers knew that when they decided they didn't want people who were carrying guns bellying up to the Statehouse bar next to them.

Wise bar owners across Ohio should follow their lead and post signs letting patrons know that guns are not welcome in their establishments. A sign won't stop anyone who is intent on taking a gun to a bar. But it might persuade law-abiding permit holders to leave their weapons at home, where they can't turn alcohol-induced stupidity into tragedy.

SIXTEEN

People Should Be Allowed to Carry Guns in Churches

Scott McPherson

Gun owners should be allowed to bring their guns to church, argues Scott McPherson in the following viewpoint. He contends that gun owners need to be armed at church for the same reasons they need to be armed in any other space: because criminals could attack them there. McPherson explains that churches have been targets of attack, even of shooting rampages. He suggests that more people died than necessary because no one in the pews had a gun on them to stop the shooter. McPherson maintains that a person's right to defend himself or herself should not stop at the church door; in fact, he asserts, historically Americans were required to bring guns to church so they would not be vulnerable while worshiping. He concludes that churches are no different from any other space in which Americans need to defend themselves.

McPherson is a policy adviser at the Future of Freedom Foundation, a nonprofit advocacy group that promotes social and economic policies that advance individual liberty, the free market, privacy, and small government.

If you're going to talk nonsense, the best strategy is to talk it loud, often, and to as many people as possible. Thanks to the editorial board at the *Springfield* (Missouri) *News-Leader,* there was no shortage of nonsense being spread around on February 19 [2009]. That day, on the paper's website, *a short commentary* by Curt Brown added another load to the dung heap of anti-gun hysteria.

Self-Defense Does Not Stop at the Church Door

The Arkansas state legislature recently passed a law which makes it legal for holders of concealed-carry permits to carry their guns in church, and Brown is upset about that. "I don't know about you," he writes, "but that sounds like something we would expect from Arkansas." I beg to differ. Recall that Arkansas's former governor, and recent presidential candidate, Mike Huckabee, wanted

The Arkansas legislature has passed a law allowing those who hold legal concealed gun permits to take their weapons to church.

a nationwide ban on smoking. A state whose former chief executive happily promotes such Nanny State ideas seems an unlikely place for libertarian sensibility on firearms policy.

But it is precisely that kind of sensibility that is being attacked by Brown. "I understand that about 20 states already allow people to carry guns to church, which really seems strange to me." Really? A church is a publicly accessible piece of private property, like Wendy's or Wal-Mart. I don't wish to trivialize the experience; ours is a nation of churchgoers, and clearly the event is quite important to each and every one of them, different from grabbing a burger. My point is that, as far as risk assessment goes, there is no reason why a person who carries a gun for self-defense would arbitrarily draw a line at his church's door.

As a matter of fact, the act has some history on this continent. In pre-Revolutionary America, the colonies of Connecticut, Massachusetts, Rhode Island, South Carolina, and Georgia all had laws requiring the carrying of guns . . . to church. Writes historian Clayton E. Cramer, in his essay "Colonial Firearm Regulation" (*Journal on Firearms & Public Policy*, Fall 2004), "The earliest mandatory gun carrying law [in British colonial America] is a 1619 Virginia statute that required everyone to attend church on the Sabbath, 'and all suche as beare armes shall bring their pieces, swords, pouder and shotte.'"

Churches Are Targets

Brown has singled out religious carriers for special criticism, but my suspicion is that what he's really upset about is that anyone would carry a gun—anywhere, anytime. According to the award-winning research of criminologist Gary Kleck, Americans use guns to defend themselves and others about 1.5 million times each year, in all kinds of scenarios and locations. One example of this comes from the state of Colorado, where in 2007 an armed security guard killed a rampaging gunman . . . in a church. Those who carry handguns wish to be able to defend themselves, and their family and friends—anywhere, anytime. Given the number of attacks on churches in recent years—a Google search using the

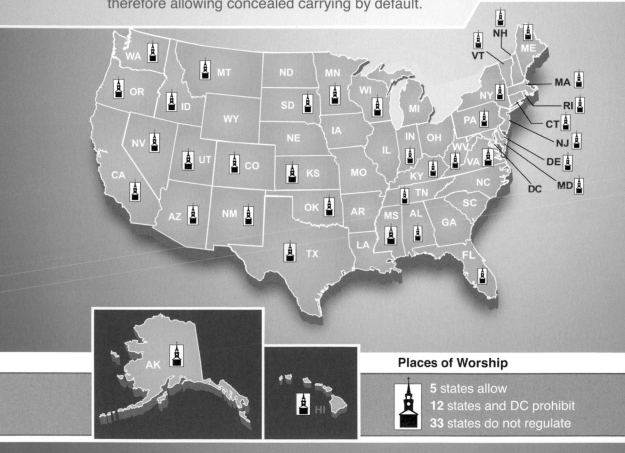

Guns in Places of Worship

A yellow icon indicates that state law generally allows the concealed carrying of a firearm by a permit holder in that location. If an icon is not present, concealed carrying is generally prohibited in that location. A white icon indicates that state law is silent in this area, therefore allowing concealed carrying by default.

Places of Worship

5 states allow
12 states and DC prohibit
33 states do not regulate

Taken from: Legal Community Against Violence, *Guns in Public Places*, July 5, 2011.

words "gunman attack church" returned about 482,000 hits—it is not unreasonable that some gun owners concerned about the safety of themselves and their family would want to slip a pistol behind their waistbands on the way to worship.

We should keep in mind, however, that under principles of private property, the churches themselves are free to establish their own policies on guns in church. If a particular church decides to ban guns, then people who attend services there must either comply with the policy or go elsewhere.

Ready to Repel Evil

There are literally millions of Americans from about 40 states who have been issued a license to carry a concealed handgun, and they consistently show themselves to be decent, peaceful, law-abiding people. Vermont and Alaska don't even require a license; one need only be a U.S. citizen to carry a gun. These states are typically the least crime-prone in America.

Curt Brown would have us believe that the new Arkansas law will lead to bloodshed. Quite the contrary. People with violent designs will now know that there are people in church fully capable of defending themselves, which operates as a powerful disincentive to their pursuing their murderous plans. It is no slight on the sanctity of a church to be prepared to repel evil there.

SEVENTEEN

Pastoral Guidance on Conceal and Carry Law

Archdiocese of Milwaukee

> In the following viewpoint, the Archdiocese of Milwaukee, part of the Catholic Church, argues that guns should not be allowed to be brought into churches. The authors suggest that bringing weapons into places of worship is disrespectful and violates the sanctity of such buildings. Worshippers need to feel safe while they pray, but knowing a pew-mate might be armed with a violent weapon interrupts one's ability to connect serenely to God. The authors argue that Catholicism is committed to nonviolence and that Jesus preached nonviolent forms of self-defense. They conclude that guns are symbols of violence, death, and oppression and thus have no place in holy spaces.
>
> The Catholic Church established the Archdiocese of Milwaukee in 1843. It serves more than six hundred thousand Catholics in southeast Wisconsin.

On November 1, 2011, it will be legal for people in Wisconsin with valid permits to carry concealed weapons on their person. The Catholic Bishops of Wisconsin offer some thoughts, in light of Catholic teaching, to assist you, both as individuals and parish leaders, in discerning how to speak and act in regards to this new legal development.

"This one goes just about anywhere ... church, national park, town hall meeting ... as well as back-to-school night ..."

© Copyright 2009 by Jimmy Margulies and CagleCartoons.com.

First, we reflect on the true meaning of freedom. God has created us to be truly free, as we exercise our liberty to build a society of respect, justice, peace and prosperity. Both natural law and our constitutional tradition uphold this understanding of individual freedom as an intrinsic human right. This freedom includes both religious liberty and the right to self-defense. True freedom, however, is not license to do whatever we choose. Rather, it is the ability to do what we morally ought to do, to build a just society, and to glorify God who is the author of all liberty and the source of human dignity.

We are called to apply this teaching to our right to carry concealed weapons. The right to bear arms is protected under our Constitution, but like all rights, it must be exercised responsibly and in accordance with applicable laws. We are obligated to use this particular freedom with due respect for others and for the desires of those who welcome us into their homes, places of business, and other public spaces, such as churches and religious institutions.

Second, we reflect on Catholic teaching, which is committed to non-violence. While the Church has always upheld the right to self-defense, peaceful means of reconciling conflicts and differences, both as individuals and nations, is the preferred method. We think of Jesus who told His disciples "to put their sword away" rather than to act violently to defend Him in the Garden of Gethsemane (Matthew 26:52). We think of the many Catholic martyrs who suffered violence and death for the sake of the Gospel, praying for their killers as Jesus did on the cross. Some of these martyrs were actually killed in churches, such as Thomas Becket, Wenceslaus, and Josaphat.

Across the country Catholic bishops have been outspoken in their opposition to carrying guns in church, saying the Catholic Church preaches a nonviolent form of self-defense.

The Catholic Church has a long tradition of sanctuary, allowing people fleeing violence to take refuge in church buildings as a place of safety and protection. For the most part, this practice has worked well because most people respect the sacred, peaceful nature of such holy places. Indeed, when violence occurs in a Catholic church, it must be reconsecrated. Intuitively, we understand that acts of violence, destruction, and murder are antithetical to the message and person of Jesus Christ and have no rightful place in our society, especially sacred places.

Whatever an individual parish decides to do regarding its policy on concealed weapons, we ask that all people seriously consider not carrying weapons into church buildings as a sign of reverence for these sacred spaces.

Those who exercise leadership in our parishes and religious institutions should consider these factors in determining whether to prohibit concealed weapons in parishes and other buildings owned by the Church and Catholic Organizations. This decision should be firmly grounded in our teaching and made with due regard for the pastoral reality and customs of the local community. All decisions should also reflect good stewardship of parish resources and the ability to address legal issues of liability that may arise from local decisions. Thus, we encourage you to consult with your insurance carriers as you proceed, and to consider how posting signs helps pastors balance the need for reverence in sacred space with their desire for security.

Bearing witness to the Gospel always presents challenges and opportunities. We encourage you to embrace this opportunity to live the example of our Lord Jesus Christ, the Prince of Peace.

EIGHTEEN

Schools Should Be Gun-Free Zones

Colin Goddard

Colin Goddard was shot on April 16, 2007, when gunman Seung-Hui Cho opened fire on the campus of Virginia Tech, where both Goddard and Cho were students. Goddard survived, but thirty-two of his classmates and teachers did not. In the following viewpoint, Goddard argues that guns should be banned from schools. He says Cho would not have been easily stopped if a fellow student had pulled a gun on him. More likely, says Goddard, is that more people would have died by accident or in crossfire shooting. Goddard says that schools are usually very safe places, much safer than places where guns are allowed. He thinks it is wrong to respond to the problem of gun violence by adding more guns to the mix. Shooting killers like Cho is a short-term solution, says Goddard; much harder is to prevent massacres by uncovering the social and emotional pathology that causes them.

Since surviving the 2007 Virginia Tech shooting, Goddard has become a gun-violence-prevention advocate.

No, bringing guns on campus won't solve the problems of school violence.

Since getting shot almost 5 years ago at Virginia Tech, I've heard this line quite often: "If just one student at Virginia Tech would have been carrying a gun on April 6, 2007, people's lives would have been saved." I could not even understand what was happening until that first bullet hit above my knee, so the certainty of the above statement is difficult to grasp. It's easy to think "yes" when you're calmly reading the newspaper, imagining hypothetical scenarios in your head, but it's entirely different when you're in the most stressful situation of your life.

More Guns, Less Safety

School shootings are very rare, and statistically speaking, you are much safer being on a college campus than you are being almost anywhere else in Virginia. In fact, the Department of Justice finds that more than 90 percent of violent student victimizations occur off-campus, in places where concealed weapons are already allowed.

Instead of working toward putting a gun in every classroom of every college, during every hour of every day, we should be working to stop the gun that may come onto one campus, in one location for just a few minutes in the entire life of that school. When looking for solutions, we should not be reactive and just try to shoot our way out of a situation that's already happening, but we should be proactive and look at why these situations are arising in the first place. Why does our first attempt at trying to control these situations start at the point when these situations become most uncontrollable?

We know that [Virginia Tech student Seung-Hui] Cho bought his guns easily and legally despite having a history of mental illness that [should have] stopped him from doing so. Cho's record was just one of an enormous number of disqualifying mental health records missing from our National Instant Criminal Background Check System [NICS], not just from Virginia, but from across the country. Some states have submitted zero disqualifying mental

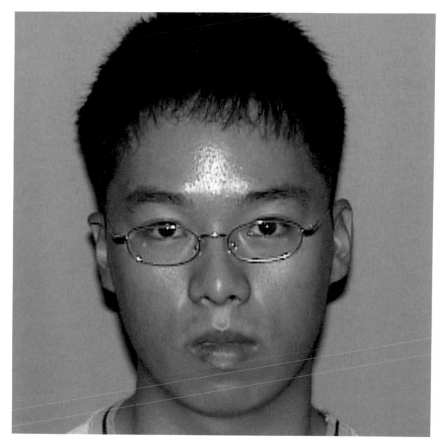

The author, one of the students shot by Seung-Hui Cho (pictured) at Virginia Tech in 2007, says that allowing guns on campus would not have stopped Cho's rampage.

health records to the NICS system—zero! Getting all the missing records into the system, then doing a background check every time someone buys a gun, would improve public safety not only on college campuses but everywhere in Virginia.

Get to the Root of the Problem

School shootings are a ritualized, dramatic and self-destructive phenomenon in America. Each instance has become a rallying cry for other tormented, isolated and suicidal kids to show the world how much they've suffered. Unfortunately in this debate, those troubled kids are being grouped into the larger category of "criminals" as if they were somehow predisposed to commit these horrible acts. They aren't being looked at as young people crying out for help. Mental health issues should be at the center of this debate and we should be discussing more ways to help Virginians in need, not just being able to shoot them. Shame on those unwilling to be their brothers' keeper, but being all too eager to be his executioner.

NINETEEN

Schools Should Not Be Gun-Free Zones

Philip Harris

> When this viewpoint was originally published in the *Mercury*, the student newspaper at the University of Texas at Dallas, Philip Harris was a student there. He discusses how in September 2010, a student opened fire on the university's main campus in Austin. Although no one was killed, Harris says that the fact that other students are not allowed to carry guns made them unnecessarily vulnerable. He says murderers do not respect the boundaries of gun-free zones. In fact, gun-free zones dangerously advertise the fact that people operating in them are unarmed, and that the shooter will have an advantage over them. If students were armed, says Harris, they would not have to wait for police to get to the scene. The armed students would already be there and could prevent much devastation if carrying guns were legal. Harris concludes that schools endanger students when they do not let them defend themselves.

On Sept. 28, [2010] math sophomore Colton Tooley opened fire with an AK-47 outside and then inside the Perry Castaneda Library at UT [University of Texas at Austin]. No one was hurt or killed, except Tooley, who took his own life.

Did somebody forget to tell Tooley the UT campus is a gun-free zone? I have been wracking my brain for the last few weeks trying to figure out how he was able to physically bring a gun onto the campus when the stated policy of the University is that students simply aren't allowed to have guns.

My sense of security at UTD [University of Texas at Dallas] has been tragically shattered. I have been banking my feelings of personal security on the fact that UTD is officially "gun-free."

Although the University of Texas at Dallas was a gun-free zone, Colton Tooley (pictured) opened fire on students with an AK-47 assault rifle and then took his own life.

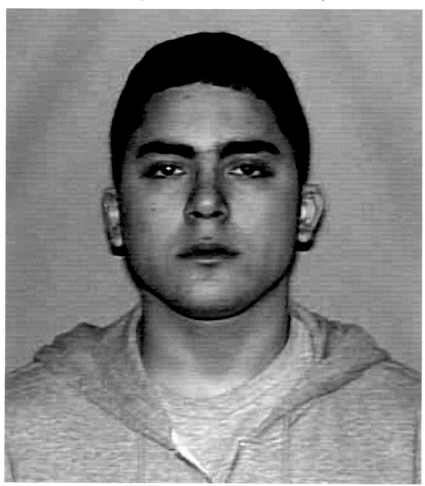

The natural conclusion to this policy seemed to be that students are physically incapable of bringing firearms onto any part of the campus. Apparently this isn't the case.

Now it's time to get real.

Gun-Free Zones Announce Vulnerability

How many tragedies have to happen or almost happen, like on the UT campus a few weeks ago, before we wake up and realize that gun-free school zones make absolutely no sense? Never before have I heard such foolish statements as when discussing gun policy on a university campus. Statements so ungrounded in logic as to be absurd.

"I just feel safer on a campus that doesn't allow guns, I like knowing that the person next to me in class doesn't have a firearm." How on earth is this a possibility? We don't attend a school surrounded by fences and metal detectors. Anybody who pleases can waltz onto campus armed to any degree they choose.

In fact, the only thing that gun-free school zones guarantee is that all of the law-abiding, responsible students at a university, and there are many, won't have a weapon. The people who break laws are the people we least want to carry a weapon, and those are the only ones who would carry a gun in a gun-free school zone. Besides the police, who are legally allowed to carry a gun, of course.

Armed Students Get There Faster than Police

Readers shouldn't misunderstand this article as critical of the police force. They work very hard to protect our campus and enforce laws. But the next most ridiculous statement I hear regarding gun-free school zones is, "It's the police's job to make campuses safe and secure, so students shouldn't be allowed to carry a gun with a concealed carry license."

The last time I checked, there isn't a police officer in every classroom on campus. That kind of a police presence might be the slightest bit overbearing, not to mention entirely impractical financially and administratively. The police are effective at enforcing laws and protecting students, but they aren't omnipresent. School shootings often lead to several tragic deaths before police can arrive and defuse the situation.

It's clear, after several school shootings in the last few years, that gun-free school zones cannot physically or realistically keep students from carrying weapons. It's nice to pretend that if a University says students can't have guns, nobody has one, but it isn't reality. Universities have harsh policies against drug and alcohol possession, but students trample all over these rules on a regular basis.

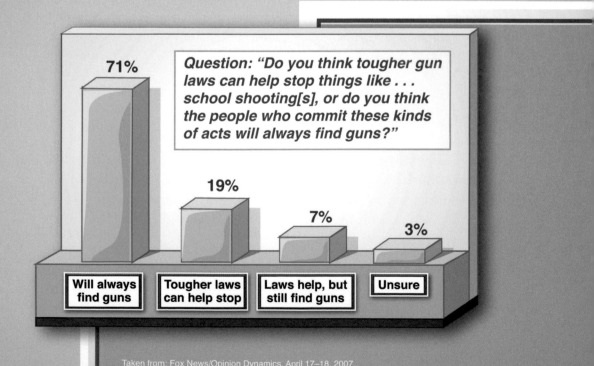

Are School Shootings Inevitable?

The majority of Americans think tighter gun control laws will not reduce the number of school shootings.

71%

Question: "Do you think tougher gun laws can help stop things like . . . school shooting[s], or do you think the people who commit these kinds of acts will always find guns?"

19%

7%

3%

| Will always find guns | Tougher laws can help stop | Laws help, but still find guns | Unsure |

Taken from: Fox News/Opinion Dynamics, April 17–18, 2007.

Banning Weapons Leaves Students Defenseless

While the UT campus [the main campus in Austin] is three hours away, the UTD campus has not been free from the possession of weapons either. This past summer a student was robbed at gunpoint after returning home from an off-campus ATM. Prior to that, a student brought a firearm onto campus claiming it as a prop, allegedly without any intent to commit a crime.

My point is not to make another tired plea for concealed carry on college campuses. While I personally believe this is a viable solution, many do not, and trying to make that point here would cause too many people to miss my point in an effort to combat the logic or wisdom of allowing college students to carry concealed weapons.

The more important conclusion is that simply banning weapons on a campus doesn't work. There have been enough school shootings to show that no matter how firm a university's rules are about weapons, no matter how many signs and postings show pictures of guns with a circle around them and a line drawn through them, students still bring guns onto campus and kill other students. New solutions must be discussed. Whether this means concealed carry, more police officers, or preventative measures to help troubled students not resort to violence, something must be done to ensure a safe campus for UTD students.

What You Should Know About Gun Violence

Facts About Gun Ownership in the United States

According to the Brady Campaign to Prevent Gun Violence:

- The United States has an estimated 283 million guns in civilian hands.
- Each year, about 4.5 million new firearms, including approximately 2 million handguns, are sold in the United States.
- An estimated 2 million secondhand firearms are sold each year as well.
- In 2009, police recovered at least 239,883 guns in connection with crimes.
- Gun owners throw away an estimated 36,000 guns every year.
- Household gun ownership has been declining since the 1970s, but personal gun ownership is on the rise. The average number of guns per owner increased from 4.1 in 1994 to 6.9 in 2004.
- Gun ownership dropped by more than 40 percent from 1977 to 2010.
- About one-third of households (32.3 percent) reported owning a gun in 2010.
- Gun ownership is highly concentrated. Approximately 20 percent of gun owners own 65 percent of the nation's guns.
- Approximately a quarter of US adults own a gun.
- Household gun ownership levels vary greatly by state, from 60 percent in Wyoming to 9 percent in Hawaii.

- The United States tops the list of countries for how many guns exist per hundred people, with ninety-seven guns per hundred people and a total estimate of up to 290,000,000 firearms.

In 2012, the Bureau of Justice Statistics and the National Institute of Justice reported the following statistics about gun violence:
- In 2005, 11,346 persons were killed by firearm violence.
- A total of 477,040 persons were victims of a crime committed with a firearm.
- Most murders in the United States are committed with firearms, especially handguns.
- In 2006, firearms were used in 68 percent of murders, 42 percent of robberies, and 22 percent of aggravated assaults nationwide.
- Nearly all gang-related homicides involve guns (97 percent).
- Nonfatal firearm-related crime accounted for 9 percent of all violent crime in 2005. These crimes include rape, sexual assault, robbery, and aggravated assault.

Landmark Supreme Court Decisions Regarding the Second Amendment

The Supreme Court has made several landmark decisions about the right to bear arms in the United States. These include:
- *United States v. Miller* (1939): Ruled that sawed-off shotguns are not constitutionally protected. Led to the development of the National Assault Weapons Act.
- *District of Columbia v. Heller* (2008): Protected a person's right to possess a firearm even if not connected to a militia, and protected the right to use the firearm for lawful purposes such as self-defense. As such, it invalidated two District of Columbia laws, one that banned handguns and one that required lawful firearms in the home to be disassembled or trigger-locked. This was the first Supreme Court decision that interpreted the Second Amendment since the 1939 *Miller* decision.

- *McDonald* v. *Chicago* (2010): Ruled that the Second Amendment is applicable to all individual states.

American Opinions of Guns

According to a 2011 *Time* magazine poll:

- 51 percent of Americans think gun control laws need to be more strict.
- 7 percent think they should be less strict.
- 39 percent think gun control laws are about right.
- 2 percent were unsure.

The poll also asked readers to rate their agreement with the following two statements:

"In order to protect the constitutional rights of gun owners, state and local governments should NOT be allowed to ban handguns and concealed weapons, even in high crime areas."

- 37 percent strongly agreed.
- 23 percent somewhat agreed.
- 15 percent somewhat disagreed.
- 23 percent strongly disagreed.
- 2 percent were unsure.

"Should the federal government be allowed to ban the sale of semiautomatic assault weapons, except for use by the military or police, or is it more important to protect the rights of gun owners to purchase any guns they wish to purchase?"

- 62 percent said allowed to ban.
- 35 percent said protect rights of gun owners.
- 3 percent were unsure.

According to a 2010 Pew Research Center poll:

- 46 percent of Americans think it is more important to protect the right to own guns.
- 50 percent think it is more important to control ownership.
- 4 percent are unsure.

According to a *New York Times* poll taken in 2011:

- 46 percent of all Americans think gun control laws should be more strict.
- 13 percent think they should be less strict.
- 38 percent think they should remain as they are.
- 3 percent are unsure.

- 27 percent of Republicans think gun control laws should be more strict.
- 17 percent of Republicans think they should be less strict.
- 53 percent of Republicans think they should remain as they are.
- 3 percent are unsure.

- 68 percent of Democrats think gun control laws should be more strict.
- 5 percent of Democrats think they should be less strict.
- 25 percent of Democrats think they should remain as they arc.
- 2 percent are unsure.

- 42 percent of Independents think gun control laws should be more strict.
- 17 percent of Independents think they should be less strict.
- 40 percent of Independents think they should remain as they are.
- 1 percent are unsure.

An NBC News/*Wall Street Journal* poll found:

- 52 percent of Americans think laws covering the sale of firearms should be made more strict.
- 10 percent think such laws should be less strict.
- 37 percent think such laws should be kept as they are.
- 1 percent are unsure.

A 2011 ABC News/*Washington Post* poll found:

- 48 percent support a ban on semiautomatic handguns.
- 50 percent oppose a ban on semiautomatic handguns.
- 2 percent are unsure.

- 31 percent support a ban on the sale of handguns except to law enforcement.
- 67 percent oppose a ban on the sale of handguns except to law enforcement.
- 2 percent are unsure.

- 57 percent support a ban on high-capacity ammunition clips (those that contain more than ten rounds).
- 39 percent oppose a ban on high-capacity ammunition clips.
- 3 percent are unsure.

- 29 percent think stricter gun laws are the best way to reduce violence in the USA.
- 57 percent think stricter enforcement of such laws is the best way to reduce violence.
- 5 percent think both.
- 7 percent think neither.
- 2 percent are unsure.

- 44 percent of Americans live in a house with a gun.
- 55 percent do not.
- 83 percent of Americans supported increasing federal funding to pay for a system in which people treated for mental illness would be reported to the federal gun registry database, to prevent them from buying guns.
- 15 percent opposed such a measure.
- 2 percent were unsure.

- 71 percent of Americans supported increasing federal funding to pay for a system in which people treated for drug abuse would be reported to the federal gun registry database, to prevent them from buying guns.
- 24 percent opposed such a measure.
- 5 percent were unsure.

What You Should Do About Gun Violence

The National Institute of Justice (NIJ) reports that fifteen to twenty-four-year-olds are the most likely to be targeted by gun violence, versus other kinds of violence. According to the NIJ, Americans aged fifteen to twenty-four are more likely than people of other ages to be murdered with a gun. They are also highly likely to die from gun-related violence: From 1976 to 2005, 77 percent of homicide victims aged fifteen to seventeen died from gun-related injuries. This means that teenagers and young adults not only must be vigilant against gun violence but have the most to gain from preventing it.

Preventing Gun Violence

Gun violence can be prevented in part by avoiding guns. If guns are kept in your home, never play with them or show them off to others. Ask your parents to remove ammunition from their guns and to make sure the safety is on to prevent accidents.

Young children are especially prone to becoming victims of these kinds of accidents. The Brady Campaign to Prevent Gun Violence reports that American children aged five to fourteen are killed with guns at a rate eleven times higher than the combined rates of twenty-two other, similar countries. Also, each year, accidental firearm incidents take the lives of more than three thousand children aged zero to nineteen. In 2007, for example, more preschoolers (children under age five) died from gunshot wounds (eighty-five deaths) than did law enforcement officers killed in the line of duty (fifty-seven deaths). In fact, the Centers for Disease Control and Prevention reports that the unintentional firearm-related death rate for children zero to fourteen years old is nine times higher in the United States than in twenty-five other countries combined.

Suicide Prevention

Sometimes, the gun violence experienced by young people is intentionally self-inflicted. Guns are often used by suicidal teens to end their lives. The National Institute of Justice reports that 82 percent of such suicide victims use a gun that belongs to a family member, most often a parent. In 2007, 683 teens committed suicide with a gun, and in 2008, 411 teens were injured in a suicide attempt that involved a gun. Therefore, suicidal youth who live in a home where they can access a gun are especially at risk for committing suicide with one.

According to the National Suicide Prevention Lifeline, suicide warning signs include: Talking about wanting to die or to kill oneself; looking for a way to kill oneself, such as searching online or buying a gun; talking about feeling hopeless or having no reason to live; talking about feeling trapped or in unbearable pain; talking about being a burden to others; increasing the use of alcohol or drugs; acting anxious or agitated; behaving recklessly; sleeping too little or too much; withdrawing or feeling isolated; showing rage or talking about seeking revenge; and displaying extreme mood swings. If someone you know exhibits any of these symptoms, seek help from a teacher, administrator, school counselor, parent, older sibling, or community leader. You are not betraying your friend by confiding in someone who can help them before it is too late.

If you live in a home where there is a gun, keep that information private. Never show friends where relatives' guns are kept, and do not make it public knowledge that a gun exists in your household. Avoid allowing a scenario in which a person could steal a gun from your home and use it to do harm to themselves or others—or you.

School Shootings

School shootings are horrific acts of terror and are difficult to explain or make sense of. Communities become devastated by such shootings, which paralyze schools, destroy families, and end promising, bright lives. With each tragic incident, schools, teachers, and families learn more about the kinds of feelings, experiences, and circumstances that cause some students to turn murderous.

If you have anxiety about a shooting occurring at your school, take comfort in the knowledge that they are actually quite rare. Media reports on school shootings tend to be intense and pervasive, and sensationalized stories may give the impression that school shootings are increasingly common. Yet shootings at schools and universities remain an exceedingly uncommon event.

Between 1992 and 2012, there were 376 school shootings. While that is more than any other country in the world, and averages to more than 18 school shootings per year, school shootings are still relatively rare events, considering that there are around 125,000 public and private schools in the United States. So the chances of a shooting occurring at your school are low. The Centers for Disease Control and Prevention estimates that murders that occur during school shootings compose only 0.96 percent of the total homicides committed each year and puts the average annual homicide rate at 0.03 per 100,000 students.

The most important role you can play in preventing school shootings is to say something if you see something. Should someone say something suspicious or allude to an event or scenario in a way that makes you uncomfortable, report it immediately. Let someone know if you hear a classmate or classmates bragging about how they are going to punish people at school. If you receive a cryptic text message, e-mail, or see an online post that warns you to stay away from school on a particular day, or discusses a seemingly big event, or even one that spews a disturbing amount of hatred for a group of students or an individual, immediately tell a parent, a counselor, an administrator, or a teacher. Many dozens of school shootings have been prevented because students reported activity or information that seemed suspicious or otherwise wrong to them. In the process they have saved many lives, including possibly their own.

ORGANIZATIONS TO CONTACT

The editors have compiled the following list of organizations concerned with the issues debated in this book. The descriptions are derived from materials provided by the organizations. All have publications or information available for interested readers. The list was compiled on the date of publication of the present volume; names, addresses, phone and fax numbers, and e-mail and Internet addresses may change. Be aware that many organizations take several weeks or longer to respond to inquiries, so allow as much time as possible.

American Civil Liberties Union (ACLU)
125 Broad St., 18th Fl.
New York, NY 10004
(212) 549-2500
e-mail: aclu@aclu.org
website: www.aclu.org

The ACLU champions the rights set forth in the Declaration of Independence and the US Constitution. It interprets the Second Amendment as a guarantee for states to form militias, not as a guarantee of the individual right to own and bear firearms. Consequently, the organization believes that gun control is constitutional and necessary.

The Brady Center to Prevent Gun Violence
1225 Eye St. NW, Ste. 1100
Washington, DC 20005
website: www.bradynetwork.org

One of the premier gun control advocates in the country, the Brady Center provides numerous reports, fact sheets, and studies about the various ways in which guns hurt all sectors of society.

Citizens Committee for the Right to Keep and Bear Arms
12500 NE Tenth Pl.
Bellevue, WA 98005
(425) 454-4911
website: www.ccrkba.org

The committee believes that the US Constitution's Second Amendment guarantees and protects the right of individual Americans to own guns. It works to educate the public concerning this right and to lobby legislators to prevent the passage of gun-control laws.

Coalition to Stop Gun Violence
1424 L St. NW, Ste. 2-1
Washington, DC 20005
e-mail: csgv@csgv.org
website: www.csgv.org

The coalition lobbies at the local, state, and federal levels to ban the sale of handguns and assault weapons to individuals and to institute licensing and registration of all firearms. It also litigates cases against firearms makers and works to raise awareness about how the prevalence of guns in society contributes to violent crime.

Gun Owners of America (GOA)
8001 Forbes Pl., Ste. 102
Springfield, VA 22151
(703) 321-8585
e-mail: goamail@gunowners.org
website: www.gunowners.org

This lobbying organization supports the ownership of guns as an issue of personal freedom and is dedicated to protecting and defending the Second Amendment rights of gun owners. Its online resources include the newsletter the *Gunowners*, gun control fact sheets, information about firearms legislation in Congress, and articles that support the arming of civilians, students, and teachers in an effort to stop school shooters and other armed criminals.

Independence Institute
727 E. Sixteenth Ave.
Denver, CO 80203
(303) 279-6536
website: www.i2i.org

The Independence Institute is a think tank that supports gun ownership as a civil liberty and a constitutional right. Its publications include articles and booklets opposing gun control, many of which are found on its website.

Jews for the Preservation of Firearms Ownership (JPFO)
PO Box 270143
Hartford, WI 53027
(262) 673-9745
e-mail: jpfo@jpfo.org
website: www.jpfo.org

The JPFO is an organization that believes Jewish law mandates self-defense. Its primary goal is the elimination of the idea that gun control is a socially useful public policy.

National Alliance for Safe Schools (NASS)
PO Box 335
Slanesville, WV 25444-0335
(304) 496-8100
e-mail: nass@frontiernet.net
website: www.safeschools.org

Founded in 1977 by a group of school security directors, the NASS was established to provide training, security assessments, and technical assistance to school districts interested in reducing school-based crime and violence. It publishes the book *Making Schools Safe for Students*.

National Crime Prevention Council (NCPC)
2001 Jefferson Davis Hwy., Ste. 901
Arlington, VA 22202-4801

(202) 466-6272 • fax: (202) 296-1356
website: www.ncpc.org

The NCPC is a branch of the US Department of Justice. Through its programs and education materials, the council works to teach Americans how to reduce crime and to address its causes. It provides readers with information on gun control and gun violence.

National Institute of Justice (NIJ)
810 Seventh St. NW
Washington, DC 20531
website: www.nij.gov

A component of the Office of Justice Programs of the US Department of Justice, the NIJ supports research on crime, criminal behavior, and crime prevention. Its website contains a wealth of reliable statistical and factual information about gun violence and crimes involving firearms, including several authoritative reports.

National Rifle Association of America (NRA)
11250 Waples Mill Rd.
Fairfax, VA 22030
(703) 267-1000
website: www.nra.org

With nearly 3 million members, the NRA is America's largest organization of gun owners. The NRA believes that gun control laws violate the US Constitution and do not reduce crime.

Second Amendment Foundation
12500 NE Tenth Pl.
Bellevue, WA 98005
(425) 454-7012
website: www.saf.org

The foundation is dedicated to informing Americans about their Second Amendment right to keep and bear firearms. The foundation publishes numerous books and articles, many of which are about school shootings.

Violence Policy Center
1730 Rhode Island Ave. NW, Ste. 1014
Washington, DC 20036
(202) 822-8200
e-mail: info@vpc.org
website: www.vpc.org

The center is an educational foundation that conducts research on firearms violence. It works to educate the public concerning the dangers of guns and supports gun control measures. The center's publications include the reports *Safe at Home: How DC's Gun Laws Save Children's Lives*; *An Analysis of the Decline in Gun Dealers, 1994 to 2005*; and *Really Big Guns, Even Bigger Lies*.

Youth Crime Watch of America (YCWA)
9703 S. Dixie Hwy., Ste. 120
Miami, FL 33156
(786) 924-1650
e-mail: ycwa@ycwa.org
website: www.ycwa.org

The YCWA is a nonprofit organization that assists youth in actively reducing crime and violence in their schools and communities. Its resources include handbooks for adult advisers and youth on starting and operating a Youth Crime Watch program, a "Getting Started" video, a *Mentoring Activities* handbook, and a *Talking with Youth About Prevention* teaching guide.

BIBLIOGRAPHY

Books

Matt Doeden, USA Today's *Debate: Voices and Perspectives; Gun Control; Preventing Violence or Crushing Constitutional Rights?* Breckenridge, CO: Twenty-First Century Books, 2011.

Brian Doherty, *Gun Control on Trial: Inside the Supreme Court Battle over the Second Amendment.* Washington, DC: Cato Institute, 2009.

Richard Feldman, *Ricochet: Confessions of a Gun Lobbyist.* New York: Wiley, 2007.

John R. Lott Jr., *More Guns, Less Crime: Understanding Crime and Gun Control Laws.* 3rd ed. Chicago: University of Chicago Press, 2010.

Mark R. Pogrebin, Paul B. Stretesky, N. Prabha Unnithan, *Guns, Violence, and Criminal Behavior: The Offender's Perspective.* Boulder, CO: Lynne Rienner, 2012.

Adam Winkler, *Gunfight: The Battle over the Right to Bear Arms in America.* New York: Norton, 2011.

Periodicals and Internet Sources

Cory Booker, "'Insane' Concealed Weapons Bill Puts Cops at Risk," *Huffington Post*, October 19, 2011. www.huffington post.com/2011/10/19/cory-booker-concealed-weapons -legislation_n_1020188.html.

Brady Center to Prevent Gun Violence, "Officers Gunned Down: How Weak Gun Laws Put Police at Risk," May 2011. www .bradycenter.org/xshare/pdf/reports/Officers-Gunned-Down.pdf.

Marcus Breton, "Gun Violence Won't Be Prevented by More Gun Ownership," *Sacramento (CA) Bee*, January 16, 2011. www.mcclatchydc.com/2011/01/16/106651/commentary-gun -violence-wont-be.html.

Jimmy Carter, "What Happened to the Ban on Assault Weapons?," *New York Times*, April 27, 2009. www.nytimes.com/2009/04/27/opinion/27Carter.html.

Cincinnati.com, "Guns in Ohio Bars? Let's Not Drink to That," May 13, 2011. http://news.cincinnati.com/article/20110513/EDIT01/105150330/Editorial-Guns-Ohio-bars-Let-s-not-drink-that?odyssey=mod|newswell|text|FRONTPAGE|p.

Ken Cuccinelli, "Pistols in the Pews," *Newport News (VA) Daily Press*, April 13, 2011. http://articles.dailypress.com/2011-04-13/news/dp-edt-cuccinelli-guns-editorial-20110413_1_gun-rights-activists-gun-bills-people.

Gary Marvin Davison, "Don't Weep at Urban Violence; Prevent It with Better Schools," *Minneapolis Star Tribune*, August 30, 2011. www.startribune.com/opinion/commentaries/128713028.html?source=error.

Delaware County (PA) Daily Times, "It's Past Time to Renew Assault-Weapons Ban," April 20, 2009. www.delcotimes.com/articles/2009/04/20/opinion/doc49ebdc73b028e616920820.txt?viewmode=fullstory.

Marion Wright Edelman, "Gun Violence and Children: Have We No Respect for Life?," *Insight News*, September 18, 2010. http://insightnews.com/commentary/6528-gun-violence-and-children-have-we-no-respect-for-life.

Bonnie Erbe, "Gun Control—If Not Now, Then When?," *East Valley Tribune* (Tempe, AZ), January 12, 2011. www.eastvalleytribune.com/opinion/article_a397561e-le9b-lle0-a623-001cc4c002e0.html.

Eugene (OR) Register Guard, "A Stricken OUS Rule Needs to Be Turned Into a Law," October 2, 2011. www.registerguard.com/web/opinion/26956959-47/guns-campus-carry-gun-oregon.html.csp.

Charles Howard, "Heeding God's Call to End Gun Violence," *Huffington Post*, January 29, 2011. www.huffingtonpost.com/charles-howard/one-groups-efforts-to-hee_b_814551.html.

Ashley N. Johnson, "Gun Violence Destroying Pennsylvania's Black Community," *Black Voice News* (Riverside, CA), May 9, 2011. www.blackvoicenews.com/news/news-wire/46137-gun-violence-destroying-pennsylvania-cities-black-community.html.

Kevin Johnson, "Series of Ills Put Police at Greater Risk," *USA Today*, August 25, 2011. www.usatoday.com/news/nation/story/2011-08-25/Series-of-ills-put-police-at-greater-risk/50140186/1.

Alan Korwin, "Are Gun-Free Zones . . . Gun Free?," *American Handgunner*, September 2, 2011. www.americanhandgunner.com/are-gun-free-zones-gun-free.

Patrick Krey, "Gun Control Leads to Militarized Law Enforcement," *New American*, May 11, 2010. www.thenewamerican.com/index.php/usnews/crime/3524-gun-control-leads-to-militarized-law-enforcement.

Robert A. Levy, "Gun Control Measures Don't Stop Violence," Cato Institute, January 19, 2011. www.cato.org/pub_display.php?pub_id=12715.

John Longenecker, "Is Gun Violence an Epidemic?," *Patriot Post*, September 23, 2011. http://patriotpost.us/commentary/2011/09/23/is-gun-violence-an-epidemic.

John R. Lott Jr., "Gun-Free Zones Are Not Safe," Fox News, April 21, 2008. www.foxnews.com/story/0,2933,352006,00.html.

John R. Lott Jr., "How Obama Reduced Crime Rates Last Year," *Big Government* blog, June 8, 2010. http://biggovernment.com/jlott/2010/06/08/how-obama-reduced-crime-rates-last-year.

Heather Martens, "While We Point Fingers, Kids Are Pointing Guns," *Minneapolis Star Tribune*, August 31, 2011. www.startribune.com/opinion/otherviews/128844613.html.

National Shooting Sports Foundation, "Semi-automatic Rifle Ban Would Reduce Jobs, Not Crime," *RightSideNews*, February 26, 2009. www.rightsidenews.com/200902263807/editorial/us-opinion-and-editorial/semi-automatic-rifle-ban-would-reduce-jobs-not-crime.html.

New York Times, "An Assault on Everyone's Safety," January 11, 2011. www.nytimes.com/2011/01/11/opinion/11tue1.html?_r=2&src=dayp.

New York Times, "No Right to Bear Assault Weapons," October 10, 2011. www.nytimes.com/2011/10/10/opinion/no-right-to-bear-assault-weapons.html.

Newark (NJ) Star-Ledger, "National Right-to-Carry Reciprocity Act Would Put NJ at Risk," *BlogNJ*, September 26, 2011. http://blog.nj.com/njv_editorial_page/2011/09/national_right-to-carry_recipr.html.

Bob Owens, "The Assault Weapons Ban: How Silly Was It? (Part One)," *Pajamas Media* (blog), July 26, 2011. http://pjmedia.com/blog/the-assault-weapons-ban-how-silly-was-it-part-one/?singlepage=true.

Stafford County (VA) Sun, "Guns in Church? No Way," April 13, 2011. www2.staffordcountysun.com/news/2011/apr/13/editorial-guns-church-no-way-ar-970012.

Jim Sutherland, "Gun Free Zones from a Canadian's Perspective," *The Truth About Guns.com* (blog), July 25, 2011. www.thetruthaboutguns.com/2011/07/jim-sutherland/gun-free-zones-from-a-canadians-perspective.

USA Today, "Guns on Campus Could Harm More than Protect," February 28, 2011. www.usatoday.com/news/opinion/editorials/2011-03-01-editorial01_ST_N.htm?loc=interstitialskip.

James H. Warner, "Assault Rifle Ban on the Horizon," *Soldier of Fortune*, October 28, 2009. www.sofmag.com/2009/10/assault-rifle-ban-on-the-horizon.

Washington Post, "Time to Resurrect the Assault Weapons Ban," January 27, 2011. www.washingtonpost.com/wp-dyn/content/article/2011/01/27/AR2011012706755.html.

Henry J. Waters, "Gun Violence—Commentary," *Columbia (MO) Daily Tribune*, July 27, 2010. www.columbiatribune.com/news/2010/jul/27/gun-violence.

Kevin D. Williamson, "Assault-Weapons Ban Would Not Have Prevented the Tucson Shooting," *National Review*, January 9, 2011. www.nationalreview.com/corner/256693/assault-weapons -ban-would-not-have-prevented-tucson-shooting-kevin-d -williamson.

Adam Winkler, "The Guns of Academe," *New York Times*, April 15, 2011. www.nytimes.com/2011/04/15/opinion/15winkler .html.

Shmuly Yanklowitz, "Gun Control vs. Gun Rights," *Jewish Week*, October 25, 2011. www.thejewishweek.com/features/street _torah/gun_control_vs_gun_rights.

INDEX

African Americans, are particularly threatened by gun violence, 29–33
AK-47 assault rifle, *75*, 76
Archdiocese of Milwaukee, 89
Arizona Daily Star (newspaper), 67
Arms Trade Treaty (United Nations), 38
Assault weapons ban
seizures of assault weapons in Virginia during/after, 69
should be reinstated, 67–71
should not be banned, 72–76

Baca, Lee, *70*
Background checks, 43, 50, 52
gun lobby and, 60
gun show loophole, and 52
National Instant Criminal Background Check System (NICS) and, 94–95
support for requiring sellers at gun shows to conduct, 13

Bars
people should be allowed to carry guns in, 77–79
people should not be allowed to carry guns in, 80–83
states allowing concealed carrying of firearms in, *79*
The Bias against Guns (Lott), 16
Bishop, Amy, 20, *21*
Boxer, Barbara, *70*
Brady Campaign to Prevent Gun Violence, 5, 68, 71
Brady Center to Prevent Gun Violence, 48,
Brady Handgun Violence Prevention Act (1993), 50
Braga, Anthony, 65
Breivik, Anders Behring, 14, 15–16
Breton, Marcus, 8
Brown, Curt, 85, 86, 88

Catholic Church(es), *91*
nonviolence teachings of, 90–91
tradition of, as sanctuaries from violence, 92
Centers for Disease Control and Prevention, 41, 107, 120

Children, are particularly threatened by gun violence, 39–47
Children's Defense Fund, 39, 40
Cho, Seung-Hui, 93, 94, 95
Churches
  people should be allowed to carry guns in, 84–88
  people should not be allowed to carry guns in, 89–92
  states allowing concealed carrying of firearms in, 87
Columbus Dispatch (newspaper), 82
Conceal and carry laws, 17–18, 59–60
  pastoral guidance on, 89–92
  by state, in 1981 vs. 2011, 61
Coryell, Skip, 24
Cramer, Clayton E., 86
Crime prevention
  by armed citizens, 6
  civilian gun ownership help police in, 53–57

Dahle, Alice, 34
Deaths, firearm, 22–23
  of black male youth, 29
  of children/teens, 30, 32, 41, 41–42, 44–47, 45
  states with highest/lowest rates of, 12

in US vs. other countries, 12
Department of Justice, US, 94

Elder, Larry, 6
Evans, Harold, 7, 9

Falcone, John, 50
Federal Bureau of Investigation (FBI), 31, 79
Franks, Trent, 10
Fraternal Organization of Police, 68
Future of Freedom Foundation, 72, 84

Giffords, Gabrielle, 7–8, 11
Goddard, Colin, 93
Green, Christina, 11
Gun control laws
  can reduce gun violence, 58–62
  disarm noncriminal citizens, 74–75
  restrict those least likely to commit violence, 63–66
Gun ownership
  personal vs. by households, trend in, 28
  public support for, 17, 26
  rates of, by country, 22
  states with highest/lowest rates of, 12

is on decline in US, 28
in US, 5
Gun violence
  is particular threat to
    African Americans,
    29–33
  is particular threat to
    children, 39–47
  is particular threat to
    women, 34–38, 35
  is product of sick society,
    19–23
  tighter gun control laws
    can reduce, 58–62
Guns
  cause violence, 9–13
  in homes, murder risk and,
    36
  people should be allowed to
    carry in bars, 77–79
  people should be allowed to
    carry in churches, 84–88,
    85
  people should not be
    allowed to carry in bars,
    80–83
  people should not be
    allowed to carry in
    churches, 89–92
  prevent violence, 14–18
  should be banned from
    schools, 93–96
  should not be banned from
    schools, 97–101
  a society without, is sick,
    24–28

Gun show loophole, 52
  support for closing, 13
Gun-free zones
  are havens for crime, 54
  schools should be, 93–96
  schools should not be,
    97–101

Harris, Philip, 97
Heller, Charles, 68
Homicide rates
  black, 32–33
  by race/gender, 31
  by race/manner, 30
  in US *vs.* other countries,
    12
Hornberger, Jacob, 72
Huckabee, Mike, 85–86

Jacocks, Jake, Jr., 78
Jesus, 91, 92

Kates, Don B., Jr., 63
Kennedy, David, 65
Keynes, John Maynard,
    77
Kleck, Gary, 86

Lee, Mike, 10
Lott, John R., Jr., 16–17
Loughner, Jared Lee, 7–8
Love, David A., 19
Luntz, Frank, 13

Martin, Trayvon, 7, 40

Mayors Against Illegal
  Guns, 13
Mbambi, Annie Matundu,
  36
McDonnell, Bob, 78
McGinness, John, 8
McPherson, Scott, 83
Mixon, Lovelle, 63, 64,
  66
More Guns, Less Crime
  (Lott), 16
Murderers, percentage with
  previous criminal records,
  65

National Academy of
  Sciences, 56
National Association of
  Police Organizations,
  68
National Coalition to Ban
  Handguns, 65
National Instant Criminal
  Background Check System
  (NICS), 94–95
National Institute of Justice,
  6
National Rifle Association
  (NRA), 10, 13, 58, 69
National Right-to-Carry
  Reciprocity Act (proposed,
  2011), 43, 60, 62
National Sheriffs'
  Association, 68
New York Times
  (newspaper), 65, 73, 76

NICS (National Instant
  Criminal Background
  Check System), 94–95
NRA (National Rifle
  Association), 10, 13, 58, 69

Obama, Barack, 13, 20, 77, 78
Opinion polls. *See* Surveys

Palmer, Tom, 57
Police officers
  civilian gun ownership
    helps, 53–57
  states with killings of,
    during 2010, *51*
  support for gun laws
    among, 13
  widespread gun ownership
    is risk to, 48–52, *49*
The Politics of Gun Control
  (Spitzer), 70
Polls. *See* Surveys
Protection of Lawful
  Commerce in Arms Act
  (2005), 52
Prunty, Timothy, 49

Rand Corporation, 71
Reagan, Michael, 14, *15*
Reynolds, Glen, 57
Richmond Times-Dispatch
  (newspaper), 78

Schools
  opinion on tighter gun
    control as means to
    reduce shootings in, *100*

PICTURE CREDITS